Theophrastus
THE CHARACTERS

Menander
PLAYS AND FRAGMENTS

TRANSLATED BY

PHILIP VELLACOTT

PENGUIN BOOKS
BALTIMORE · MARYLAND

Penguin Books Ltd, Harmondsworth, Middlesex, England
Penguin Books Inc., 3300 Clipper Mill Road, Baltimore, Md 21211 U.S.A.
Penguin Books Australia Ltd, Ringwood, Victoria, Australia

—

First published 1967, except for *The Bad-Tempered Man* (first
published by Oxford University Press 1960)

—

Copyright © Philip Vellacott, 1967
The Bad-Tempered Man copyright © Oxford University Press, 1960

—

Made and printed in Great Britain by
Hazell Watson & Viney Ltd
Aylesbury, Bucks
Set in Monotype Bembo

The terms for performance of these
translations may be obtained from the League of Dramatists,
84 Drayton Gardens, London SW10, to whom all
applications for permission should be made

CONTENTS

INTRODUCTION

THEOPHRASTUS lived from 371 to 287 B.C., and Menander
from 343 to 291. Thus when Theophrastus was a young man
the last struggle for Greek independence was still at its height,
and the greatness of Athens was still living in the leadership of
Demosthenes; but Menander passed his whole life as a citizen
of a subject State. By 338 Philip of Macedon had brought the
whole of Greece under his authority. His son Alexander the
Great died in 323 in Babylon. During Alexander's long absence in the East, Antipater, one of his generals, was his regent
in Macedon and Greece; on Alexander's death Antipater became king. When he died in 319 a military struggle took place
between his son Cassander and Polyperchon, who was Antipater's nominee for the succession (see Character 8). This dis-
turbed political background seems to be taken for granted as a
normal condition of life by the people we meet both in the
Characters and in Menander's plays. The men and women de-
picted by these two writers seem to have devoted themselves
entirely, so long as actual fighting kept at a reasonable distance, to the business of the moment – to their shopping, their
gossiping, their borrowing and lending, eating and drinking,
dressing and money-making, going to law, marrying, loving
and quarrelling. The *Characters* and the plays give us innumer-
able glimpses of this vivid and varied life as it was lived by the
great-grandchildren of the men who, in the age of Euripides
and Aristophanes, fought the desperate battles of the Peloponnesian War. Menander's contemporaries were perhaps, as
individuals, not of inferior quality; but there was no longer
the cause of freedom or the glory of Athens to turn them into
heroes. On their tragic stage they revived the heroic dramas
of the fifth century; in Comedy they were concerned with
emotions of the home and the street, with slaves and sweet-
hearts, with dreams of wealth and fantasies of romance.

The author of the *Characters* was, it is said, one Tyrtamos, a native of Lesbos. Tyrtamos came to Athens to be a pupil of Aristotle; on Aristotle's death he succeeded him as head of the Lyceum, his school of philosophy in Athens; and it was Aristotle who gave him the name Theophrastus, which means 'divine speaker'. There are many passages in later writers both Greek and Latin, and particularly in Cicero, testifying to the style and eloquence which earned him this name. He was, like his master, a prolific writer on many subjects, including Rhetoric – which simply means the art of language. So it is curious that the *Characters*, his only surviving work (apart from a few quotations), shows nothing at all of the quality for which he was famous. The interest of these short pieces lies in their author's observation and selection of material. The Greek is sometimes obscure or inelegant, the vocabulary colloquial, the style unvaried and abrupt. Their terseness suggests notes for lectures, and they can hardly have been written for separate publication as a literary work. Though they have begotten in modern European literature a whole *genre* of 'character-writing' (famous imitators include La Bruyère, John Earle, and Ben Jonson), they stand in the ancient world as a unique book, and one whose purpose is not at first apparent.

There exists a Preface which is certainly not by Theophrastus; it is printed here at the end of the *Characters*. The writer of this Preface says that the work is the fruit of his study of human character 'both good and bad'. All the surviving Characters clearly come under the heading 'bad'; so it seems probable that the writer of this Preface had before him not only our *Characters* but a set of 'good' ones as well. He goes on, with naïve banality, to say that he has written these pieces for the moral instruction of the younger generation. This certainly does not ring true. The *Characters* have very little in them that could be called moral or ethical principle. They describe deviations from accepted standards of behaviour, some vicious, others comic; but they make no attempt to trace them to their causes. We may dismiss the suggestion that they formed a part of any serious work on ethics.

The most probable view is that they were written as an illustrative appendix to a work on the writing of Comedy. The wide gulf that divides Menander's comedy from that of Aristophanes makes it probable that many minds were exercised during that half-century over the nature of comedy, and that many experiments must have led to nothing, before the new and living form emerged. Menander is traditionally referred to as a pupil of Theophrastus; certainly he learnt 'divine speech', from whatever source. Both authors record with the same zest many features of everyday life in fourth-century Greece – for example, the incorrigible habit of borrowing everything, from clothing to kitchen-utensils. At the same time the connexion of the *Characters* with Aristophanes is equally close; perhaps even closer, since Aristophanes, being a creator of fantasy, can exaggerate, where Menander, committed to a degree of realism, must preserve balance. Theophrastus' descriptions are thorough-going and relentless, providing in each case the full data for a type; whereas Menander, the creator of individuals, would select, modify, present contradictions, and all with a gentle human appreciation which was no part of the purpose of Theophrastus.

Each Character begins with a definition of the abstract quality described, and proceeds to a detailed portrait of the person, his habits and his conversation. In eight of them (nos. 1, 2, 3, 6, 8, 10, 28, 29) the MSS attach an ending which is certainly a later addition. Most of these endings are feeble or pointless, and I have omitted from the translation all except that of no. 8, which is the longest, and will serve as an example. The authenticity of the opening definitions is also in doubt. They may well have been put in (as Ussher[1] suggests) by some one who thought he was dealing with a work on ethics. In a work on comedy they seem out of place; and some of

1. R. G. Ussher, *The Characters of Theophrastus*, 1960.

them are largely irrelevant to the descriptions which follow.

For the rest, the Characters can speak for themselves. This at least we owe to the writer of the spurious Preface, that we know that one half of the work – the 'good' Characters – is missing; so we need not put down Theophrastus as the jaundiced observer he might otherwise seem to be. The types of men he describes (he has not included any women) should be compared with characters in Aristophanes, whose quality is to do nothing by halves; but the world they move in belongs to Theophrastus' own time, and is the same world which we find presented, with a wealth of variety and colour, in the plays and fragments of Menander.

★

Until the beginning of the twentieth century Menander was known to the modern world only as the Greek author whom Plautus and Terence adapted or imitated, and who through them set a pattern for European playwrights eighteen centuries later; a name to conjure with in the ancient world, where he was considered unique – 'Menander cut down to half-size' was Julius Caesar's phrase for Terence, and it was probably intended as a judicious compliment. When, some sixty years ago, a papyrus was discovered in Egypt containing large portions of *Epitrepontes* (*The Arbitration*), *Periceiromene* (*The Unkindest Cut*), and *Samia* (*The Samian Woman*), it was at once recognized that Menander's reputation was well earned. These fragments from the work of his maturity showed all that had been expected in character-drawing, interest of situation, handling of plot, and sparkle of wit. *Dyskolos* (*The Bad-Tempered Man*) was discovered in 1955, and is the only complete play we have. It was produced in 317 B.C., when Menander was twenty-five, and was awarded a prize; but it is not a play of the same calibre as the later ones now known to us. The moralizing which in later fragments flows with grace and truth, here fumbles and prates; and there is a notable lack both of subtlety and of tenderness. By the time Menander was forty he had learnt what he wanted to say and how to say it; but an author's early work has a special interest, and in the case of *Dyskolos* this is enhanced by its completeness.

'Imagine that this place is Phyle in Attica.' So *Dyskolos* begins. There must have been some in that first Athenian audience who responded to this innocent invitation with a flash of memory which would have been bitter if it had been more recent. As it was eighty-seven years old it could be dismissed before Pan began to describe the sour-tempered old farmer who was to be the butt of the entertainment; but for a moment the name Phyle might well arouse sad reflections on the very character of that entertainment, so different from the bold, libertine tradition which it had replaced three generations earlier. Those who, like Callippides and his family in the play, sometimes went picnicking at Phyle would very likely sit to enjoy their lunch in the shade of fine stone walls which must still have shown traces of their military use. In 403 B.C., the year after the final defeat of Athens by Sparta and the destruction of the Long Walls, during the dismal period of the first Spartan puppet government, the oligarchical Thirty – in that solstice of despair a group of stout-hearted democrats under Thrasybulos had held out for six months in a little fortress at Phyle in Attica, in the hilly country fifteen miles to the north of the city; they had repulsed two military expeditions, and had left their stronghold only after gaining by negotiation a fair measure of that democratic principle for which they had fought.

They were men who had known Aristophanes and the breath of freedom. By their resolute courage they were able to preserve some of the civic and political values of undefeated Athens. But Athenian Comedy, as Aristophanes had created it, died with the peace; and now, after three generations, a new product was taking shape, a new species in the world of the theatre; one which belonged to the afternoon of

Athens as unmistakably as Aristophanes belonged to the mid-day, yet was destined to do what Aristophanes could not do – to take its place beside the great tragedians in guiding the development of drama, not only for four or five centuries in the ancient Mediterranean world, but for a similar period in what we call modern Europe. This was due principally to the genius of Menander; and we should remember this, and not allow the obvious comparison with his great predecessor to obscure his very different qualities.

The heart of an Aristophanes comedy was its Chorus. The fifth-century Chorus symbolized the Athenian citizen's knowledge that there was nothing he dared not think; that what he thought, he was ready to say not merely in private but in the hearing of all his fellow-citizens; and that he was no less prepared to hear what his fellow-citizen had to say, whether he liked it or not. In the Parabasis the poet voiced his own mind, and many other people's, on current topics of manners, personalities, politics and literature, without fear of reprisal either from the State or from his neighbours. The story of the play, however amusing in itself, was constructed primarily as a vehicle for satire; and the satire was crystallized in the Chorus. In Menander's day that trenchant liberty was as remote a memory as the once gallant fame of Phyle. His plays have no Chorus in the old sense. Their scenes are divided by interludes indicated in the MSS merely by the word *Chorou*, a performance 'of the Chorus'; and this performance seems to have been left to the imagination, interests, or resources of the producer.

If the Chorus was the heart of a comedy by Aristophanes, its flesh was the story – in the whole fantastic range of that rare imagination. In those plays the audience are led by the hand in two lines from Hellas to Hades, from Athens to Cloud-Cuckoo-Land, from a law-court to Socrates' 'thinking-shop'. From the outset the 'ordinary citizen' finds himself inescapably on the stage and deeply involved, holding urgent conversation with generals, politicians, wasps, birds, sausage-sellers, landladies, frogs, clouds, gods, poets, and slaves, all of immediate relevance in a unified world of intelligent non-sense. Since then more than one world had come and gone; and Alexander the Great was dead. Menander's Phyle contains only what Menander's audience saw when they went there hunting or picnicking – cottages, a spring, a shrine, and country people looking askance at trippers from the town. Imagination gives place to observation, fantasy to realism. The predicament of humble obstinate humanity in the organized State, protesting against wars and taxes and regulations and the power of money, is replaced by the predicament of the ordinary husband, son or lover, who in a world complicated by multifarious division into hostile camps – rich and poor, slave and free, old and young, native and foreign, and above all male and female – struggles through mischance and bewilderment to be in some degree faithful both to himself and to his neighbour; in other words, to achieve on the domestic level that same ideal of *dike* which the men and women of Tragedy sought on the heroic level.

Before we look further into this larger subject, it is worth while – since our one complete play is so recent a discovery, and at least one notable fragment has come to light since – to say something about the progress from the discovered papyrus to the stage performance. The manuscript of *Dyskolos* is in closely written lines with no division between words, and little punctuation. A change of speaker is indicated by a short stroke below the first letter of the line in which the change occurs, and generally, but not always, by a double point at the end of a speech; in some places the stroke is found above instead of below the line. The names of speakers are given only here and there, apparently with the intention of showing where a character enters the dialogue; but there are many evident mistakes. There are no stage-directions of any kind, except a single word (on page 77) meaning 'plays the flute'.

The process of discovering the entrance and exit of a character, of deciding who is on stage at a given moment, may be intricately involved with the establishment of the text. Each leaf of the papyrus is damaged in one or more places, and defective lines have to be completed, if this seems possible; while in undamaged lines there are fairly frequent corruptions, and opinions differ as to the correct restoration. The discarding of one hypothesis may lead to endless revision of other passages. This part of the work is the province of the textual specialist, involves prolonged and arduous research, and can move only gradually towards completion as different scholars contribute their answers to the numerous problems which arise.

One example of these will be enough: the problem of the half-dozen nameless characters. The most important of these is Cnemon's daughter, who appears among the dramatis personae but is given no name. She is allotted a few lines in Scene 1 and again in Scene 4. The name Myrrhine (a common name in Menander) does not appear anywhere in full, but on page 91, where the papyrus is torn, Cnemon addresses '... rhine and Gorgias'. At the time both his wife and his daughter are present; and it is certainly more likely that he is here addressing his wife, especially as elsewhere he consistently ignores his daughter. But for the purpose of an English production a name is entirely necessary for Cnemon's daughter, and unnecessary for his wife. So I have let Sostratos woo her as Myrrhine.

Then there is Sostratos' mother. She unquestionably appears on the stage, for Sostratos speaks to her in line 867. At the beginning of Scene 3 there are several separate lines which seem to fit neatly the character already given her by both Sostratos and Getas. Yet she is given no name; she is not included in the dramatis personae; and not a word is allotted to her.

Her dubious position is shared by her daughter and by the mother of Gorgias. At line 842 this daughter is betrothed to Gorgias, and it seems reasonable to assume that she is present on the stage at that moment. She plainly would arrive with her mother; and it is possible that she is the Plangon who is told to hurry. Gorgias' mother, who also is denied a place in the dramatis personae, is equally surely on the stage at line 867, where Sostratos presents her, and Cnemon's daughter, to his mother. But there is no line in the manuscript which can suitably be assigned to her. The opening of Scene 3 also gives us two other shadows: the flute-girl Parthenis; and the person who rudely complains that Sostratos' mother has kept everyone waiting. The latter surely cannot be the family slave Getas, and must therefore be a guest; though it is possible that Sostratos' mother is not on stage at all, and that the complaint is made by Sicon the cook to Getas.

*

Menander in the course of his fifty-two years wrote more than a hundred plays. Of this output the plays and fragments we now possess amount to about five per cent; so that, while we may feel that we have a fair idea of his style and language, we cannot pretend to guess whether the majority of his work reached or exceeded this level of quality; still less can we attempt any estimate of the range of subjects he treated, or of his development as a commentator on human nature. We do know that for centuries after his death he was regarded by ancient writers with something akin to reverence, and that his plays were widely known, often performed, and constantly quoted. The Loeb edition, for example, selects well over two hundred quotations, varying from one to twenty-odd lines, taken from unidentified plays, besides a further large selection from those for which their quoters gave a reference.

What qualities make a writer an inexhaustible mine for other writers? I take at random the first four quotations from *Hamlet* that occur to me:

There is nothing either good or bad, but thinking makes it so.

There are more things in heaven and earth, Horatio, than are dreamt of in your philosophy.

Use every man after his desert, and who would 'scape whipping?

Conscience doth make cowards of us all.

Every one of these might have come from Menander (the last, indeed, is in Menander, Fragment 632, page 246). They are not, perhaps, either profound or specially dramatic; they are, as we say, 'on the nail'; that is, true and universal; and such perceptions are, we recognize, very much in place in the tragedy of *Hamlet*. Menander wrote comedies, and in his comedies such perceptions are equally in place. His commentary on life covers many fields. His tirades against matrimony ('In marriage no survivor has ever yet been known') stand side by side with the occasional picture of an ideal state of mutual trust. His observations on the possession, use, and pursuit of money, on pride of birth, on the decay of quality, on the prosperity of the wicked or the inevitability of sorrow, on old age or friendship, on the impartiality of chance, on gratitude, guilt, servility, giving advice, getting drunk, and a hundred other topics, all show that combination of directness of thought with limpidity of expression which we are apt to call Shakespearian. Menander was not a tragedian; he did not present man face to face with time and the cosmos, with death and the depths of his own soul; but he was a poet of humanity, with an eye of genius both for detail and for the universal in human experience, and an ability on occasion to reach greater heights, such as may be seen in Fragments 481 and 552. If our five per cent remnant contains jewels like these, what a treasure must have been lost!

It is unfortunate that the term by which Menander is technically referred to is 'the comic poet'; such a phrase can only be misleading to the general reader. He is an endlessly entertaining writer; but only a small proportion of his entertainment can be called 'funny'. The greater part of it is comedy of character, which entertains by portraiture from life. The development from the stock figures of *Dyskolos* to the portraits given in *The Arbitration* and *The Samian Woman* is remarkable. Sostratos and Gorgias are simple types with little individuality; Cnemon at least reacts to experience, but cannot gain sympathy; the pretty girl in the story has virtually no existence; the fun is provided chiefly by the vivacity of the slaves. *The Arbitration*, on the other hand, immediately introduces us to an individual: Smicrines is a businessman with a legal turn of mind; as the father of the young wife in the story he might well be a stock figure; but the fragments we have of his conversation suggest that he is no more a stock figure than – to choose a Shakespearian counterpart – Polonius. In *The Samian Woman* Demeas, as an over-indulgent father and a somewhat obtuse and censorious husband, may be called a stock figure; but his remarkable mixture of unlikely qualities – he is priggish, sincere, egocentric, fussy, violent, cruel, tender-hearted, all in less than half of the play – makes him as close a parallel to Capulet as could be found anywhere. Slaves, like Onesimos in *The Arbitration*, we may naturally expect to be stock figures, since they are there largely to lay crazy plots, speak out of turn, get beaten and call each other names; but Onesimos has a quite personal selection of qualities to distinguish him: an itch for meddling, a preoccupation with dodging trouble, a delight in philosophical discourse and psychological diagnosis, a susceptible heart for the kind guitar-girl whom he in turn lets down, champions in her absence, mistrusts, and bargains with. Yet another surprise is offered in the small fragment of *The Farmer*, which opens with a sympathetic picture of a slave in love; while it is hard to believe that the Parmenon (certainly a slave's name) to whom Fragment 481 was spoken was one whom we could think of as a stock figure.

Besides the penetration of his commentary on life and the skill and variety of his character-drawing, there is a third quality in Menander which helps to explain the unique position given to him as a writer in the ancient world. This is the claim which he makes, albeit with a disarming diffidence, to be in some sense a successor to the tragedians, and in particular to Euripides. It is true that of the plays of his maturity there are only three of which we possess a substantial part; but the general character of the hundreds of short fragments supports the supposition that these three plays are typical of his work. When we find, therefore, that these plays, while various in their setting, characters, and plot, all deal with the same moral theme, we are surely justified in concluding that this theme was one which especially interested Menander; and we may perhaps go further and say it was a theme which evidently interested his audience. By many references to tragedy, and by quotations, especially from Euripides, Menander shows his familiarity and sympathy with tragic themes and with a reflective approach to moral situations.

Man's thoughts about the problem of living with his neighbour and his family are all included in the Greek word *dike*, which means 'right' or 'justice'. Many of the most famous tragedies are stories of revenge; and revenge is simply the crudest way of seeking justice. These stories (as in Aeschylus' Oresteian Trilogy, or Euripides' *Medea*) usually show the act of revenge as being more wicked than the crime which provoked it; and the result is that the feud continues. In only two plays of Euripides do we find a more hopeful solution to the problem of a wrong which has been inflicted. The final scene of *Alcestis* at least leaves a possibility that Alcestis has forgiven her husband Admetus; and in the final scene of *Hippolytus* Theseus receives full absolution and forgiveness from the son whom he cursed. But *Alcestis* is largely comedy; and Euripides did not, so far as we know, ever again after *Hippolytus* show forgiveness in action, though his characters often reproach those who refuse to forgive.

In each of the three mature plays of Menander which remain to us, a woman of good character and sympathetic personality is hastily misjudged and wronged by a husband or lover. In the first two the man recognizes his mistake, reproaches himself bitterly, and by sincere and practical repentance earns forgiveness; in the last, the MS breaks off at the point where the man has discovered his mistake, but is not yet alive to the seriousness of the wrong he has committed – though his character has been sufficiently established for us to feel sure that his awakening will not be long delayed. The actual bestowing of forgiveness has survived only in *The Unkindest Cut*; but it is performed there with a subtle charm that removes all embarrassment – a finesse of which the author of *The Bad-Tempered Man* gave little promise.

Now, of course, the making-up of a quarrel is an easy and obvious theme for comedy; and it might be said that to compare Menander's tales with those of Euripides is making much out of little. It is true that Menander works on the domestic level, not on the heroic; but both levels concern humanity (Euripides himself did not despise the domestic level), and there are several indications that Menander took seriously this aspect of his writing. First, there is the large number of surviving quotations which attest a deep concern with the human condition. Secondly there are his own frequent references to Tragedy, often implying a – perhaps self-deprecatory – claim to be similarly concerned with the real predicaments of human life. A third pointer is the whole structure of *The Arbitration*; and a fourth is a short passage in *The Unkindest Cut*. Let us look particularly at the last two.

In the first surviving scene of *The Arbitration* two slaves ask a passing citizen to settle a dispute for them. This might seem at first to an English reader somewhat far-fetched; but Theophrastus corrects this impression – see Characters 5 and 24, which show that such appeals, even to a casual passer-by, were an everyday matter. This fact in itself, as well as the important place that litigation held in the average citizen's life, reflects the passionate interest Greeks felt in questions of right and wrong. When Syriscos argues

> Justice ought to prevail
> Everywhere and on all occasions. The passer-by
> Ought to feel it's his duty to see justice done,

Daos, who has the weaker case, derides him as a 'speechifier', but the educated citizen Smicrines takes him seriously and accepts the position of arbiter. Even though the actual point in dispute – the possession of the birth-tokens – is not at the centre of the plot, the issue of just dealing certainly is. The characters are convinced that a just solution exists, and are determined to find it.

Next we see the slave Onesimos in a quandary. He has in his possession the ring found with the exposed child, which he recognizes as the ring his master lost nine months ago. Is he to show it to Charisios or not? He consults the guitar-girl Habrotonon; and his selfish mistrustfulness lights up the goodness of the slave-prostitute. She, in her exit-line, invokes a deity who has been one of the principal handmaids of *dike* ever since *The Eumenides*, and who has already in this play presided unseen over the arbitration between Syriscos and Daos:

> Holy Persuasion, help me! Bring my words success!

Hasty-tempered free-born men may go about trying to impose solutions by force; the slave-girl, whose only resources are her kind heart and a belief in right, appeals to Persuasion.

The central scene of this play is in Act 4, where first Onesimos reports the agonized self-reproach of Charisios, and then Charisios himself appears, to tell us of his wife Pamphile's nobleness of mind, contrasted with his own unjust thoughts of her.

> After myself doing what I did . . .
> I was such a brute and savage that I neither felt,
> Nor offered her, one shred of forgiveness – although she
> Had suffered the very wrong that I was guilty of.

A few lines later, when Habrotonon and Onesimos come to

bring him the information that will deliver him from his misery, he blunders straight into injustice again, hits Onesimos and threatens Habrotonon. Unhappily the MSS fail us before the scene ends. Then in Act 5, because this is a comedy, the last word on justice is given to Onesimos, who delivers an admirable sermon to Smicrines, exhorting him to deserve a happy life.

ONESIMOS: Smicrines, do you consider
   It right for a man to take his daughter from her husband?
SMICRINES: Right? No one says it's right; but in this case it's
   necessary.
ONESIMOS [*appealing to audience*]: You see? This chap reckons
   what's wrong is necessary.

Greeks in general were a passionate, revengeful, unjust race; but they knew what they were doing, and reverenced justice even while they outraged it. Onesimos' banter assumes a vital moral awareness in his audience.

The Unkindest Cut gives us a similar picture. Polemon, the hot-tempered soldier, is torn with love and with penitence for his cruel act; there is again a legally-minded older man, Pataicos, to set the rights and wrongs of the matter in perspective; and Polemon is told that the way to win back Glycera's love is not by taking the law into his own hands, but 'by persuasion'. Glycera, trying to make up her mind to forgive Polemon, finds herself face to face with her long-lost father, who now remembers with shame the selfishness which had made him expose his children in infancy. Glycera forgives her father; and in her happiness at the reunion is anxious to forgive Polemon too, since she has learnt from Pataicos how contrite he is. Pataicos says to her,

   When you've enjoyed good fortune, to be ready then
   To accept honest amends – that proves you a true Greek.

There is a moving irony in this; for if history proved anything about the 'true Greek' character, it was that Greeks chose revenge rather than forgiveness. But Menander is not being ironical. He reserves irony – of the gentlest kind – for Glycera's line,

> And that, of course, is why I forgive you!

She thus improves on Pataicos' picture of true Greek generosity, by cancelling his clause, 'When you've enjoyed good fortune'; and shows that she would have forgiven Polemon in any case, for love. The exact subtlety of these exchanges is comedy in the sense which we call Shakespearian.

This belief is an ideal of *dike* – the conviction that it is possible to find a principle of behaviour which will enable men and women to deal successfully with their own and other people's errors of impatience, ignorance or folly – this belief is a direct inheritance from the moral searchings of Aeschylus and Euripides; what is new in Menander is the application of the principle to unheroic and personal issues in common life. But between the vanishing of tragedy and the rise of Menander's comedy the search has passed through another phase.

Within ten years after the last productions of Euripides – *Orestes, Heracles, The Bacchae* – a court of Athenian *dicastae* had sat to dispense justice in the trial of Socrates, and had condemned him to death. Socrates had spent a generation and more, as a fellow-citizen of Euripides, in pursuit of the meaning of justice and goodness. During the generation after his death, Plato recorded and developed this pursuit in *The Republic*. In the generation after that, Plato's pupil and critic Aristotle took up the trail. He classified different types of justice; he distinguished the bond that joins a friend with a friend, from that which joins son to father or husband to wife; he distinguished guilt for a wrong done in anger from guilt for a wrong done with malice aforethought, or unwittingly, or against the better judgement of a good disposition. Menander was a pupil of Aristotle's successor Theophrastus; and when Charisios refers to himself as a 'student of ethics', or Onesimos with mock-pomposity proposes 'essay-questions' in the theory of behaviour, we can see the line of inheritance clearly drawn. Aristotle's studies were written down, not primarily for the guidance of lawyers or litigants, but for the intellectual and emotional satisfaction of thoughtful men who found it natural to reflect about their own moral instincts and the society in which they lived. Such men were in Menander's audience, probably in a larger proportion than would be found in a theatre audience today; and what Menander had studied under his teachers he gave to his audience, translated into living terms, in the conversation of Comedy.

*

Lastly, a word about Menander's metre. Most of his dialogue is written in a relaxed form of the same six-beat line that the tragic poets use. A longer line of eight beats, also found in Tragedy, is used by Menander in several extant passages; and near the end of *Dyskolos* appears a seven-beat line peculiar to comedy. In each case the metre is approximately reproduced in the English translation.

*

For the *Characters* of Theophrastus I have used the text and commentary of R. G. Ussher (Macmillan 1960). For the four principal fragments of Menander I have used the text and commentary of E. Capps (Ginn 1910), with some help from the text of F. G. Allinson (Loeb Library 1921). The translation of *Dyskolos* was made soon after the publication of the first text of the play, with the special purpose of a sound-radio production. This consideration influenced to some extent decisions about the allocation of parts; lines tend to be broken up among different speakers more often than is warranted by the exact balancing of probabilities which scholars have since had time to carry out. I do not feel, however, that these liberties at any point give a false impression either of the Greek text or of the play as a whole; I have therefore left them as they stand. I received at the time much generous help from Mr Raymond Raikes as Producer and from Professor Hugh Lloyd-Jones. I have also been helped by Mr E. W. Handley's edition (Methuen 1965) to make a few desirable alterations. Finally, I am deeply indebted to Mr Handley for his kindness in supplying me with his detailed notes on *The Sicyonian*.

I also acknowledge with thanks permission kindly granted by the Editor of The Loeb Classical Library and by the Harvard University Press to quote twelve lines from page 448 of the Loeb edition of Menander.

P. H. V.

Theophrastus

THE CHARACTERS

Irony, if summarily defined, would appear to be an affectation of the worse in word and deed.

The ironical man is one who goes up to people he detests and is ready to chat with them without any sign of dislike. He praises to their face men whom he has attacked behind their backs, and sympathizes with them when they are meeting ill-success. He is indulgent towards those who slander him, and unconcerned about what is being said. He talks blandly with people who are being ill-treated and who resent it. When people want to see him urgently, he tells them to come back another time. He never admits to anything he is doing, but says he is thinking of it. He pretends that he 'has only just arrived', that he 'was too late', or 'was not well'. To those who ask for a loan or a subscription he replies that he is not a rich man. When he has something to sell, he 'is not selling', and if in fact he is not selling he says he is. He pretends he didn't hear, when he did; that he hasn't seen, when he has; when he has made an admission, that he doesn't remember making it. 'I thought about that', he says; or, 'I've no idea'; or, 'That surprises me'; or, 'I once reached a similar conclusion myself.' In short, he is always using phrases of this kind: 'I don't believe it', 'I don't understand', 'You astonish me'; or, 'You give a different account of it; that wasn't the story he told *me*'; or, 'I think the whole thing's absurd'; or, 'Tell that to someone else'; or, 'I don't see how I can either disbelieve you, or condemn him'; or, 'All the same, don't be in a hurry to believe it.'

2. THE TOADY, OR FLATTERER

Flattery may be thought of as an attitude or relationship which is degrading in itself, but profitable to the one who flatters.

The toady is the sort of person who will say to the man he is walking with, 'Do you notice how people look at you? You're the only man in Athens they study in that way.' Or perhaps, 'You were being complimented yesterday in the Arcade. There was a group of thirty or more sitting talking; and the question cropped up, Who was our best citizen? Starting from that, we all came back finally to your name.' While he is going on like this, he picks a stray thread off the other's cloak; or if a bit of chaff has blown into his hair, he takes it out, and says with a laugh, 'Look at that! Because I haven't seen you for two days, you've got a beard full of grey hairs; though, if anyone's hair keeps its colour in spite of years, yours does.' Then he will tell the company to keep silent while the great man is speaking; he will praise him when he is listening; and when he pauses in his talk he will back him up with 'Hear, hear!' When his patron makes a feeble joke he laughs, stuffing his cloak into his mouth as if he couldn't contain his merriment. He asks people they meet in the street to wait until 'He' has passed. He buys apples and pears, brings them in and gives them to the children when their father is watching, kisses them and says, 'Well, youngsters, you've got a splendid father.' If he goes with his patron to help him buy some shoes, he remarks that the foot is more shapely than the shoe. If the other is on his way to visit some friend, the toady will run ahead and tell the friend, 'He's coming to see you,' and then turn back and say, 'I have announced you.' He is even capable of running errands, at a moment's notice, to the women's market. At a dinner-party he is the first to praise the wine, and he may be relied on to exclaim, 'How delicate your food is!' Then he picks up something from the table, and says, 'Now, isn't that choice?' He will ask his friend if he is cold and if he would like to put something more on; and while still asking he puts a wrap round him. What's more, he leans over to whisper in his ear; or, when talking to other guests, keeps glancing at their host. Then in the theatre, he will take the cushions from the slave, and himself arrange them on his patron's seat. His patron's house, he will say, is beautifully built; his land has been nicely planted; and his portrait is an excellent likeness.

3. THE CHATTERER

Chatter is the churning-out of long-winded, unconsidered talk.

The chatterer is the sort of man who sits down beside someone he doesn't know and begins by delivering a panegyric on his own wife; continues with an account of his dream of the night before; then describes in detail what he had for supper. Next, getting into his stride, he remarks how far inferior men of the present day are to the ancients; how reasonable wheat is now in the shops; how full of foreigners Athens is getting. He observes that since the Dionysia it has been good sailing weather; and that if only Zeus would send more rain it would be better for the farmers. Then he tells you what part of his land he will put down to crops next year; and how difficult it is to live; and that Damippus has set up an enormous torch at the Mysteries; and 'How many columns has the Odeion?' and 'I was violently sick yesterday'; and 'What day of the month is it today?' Then he tells you that the Mysteries are in September, the Apaturia in October, and the Rural Dionysia in December. In fact, if you put up with him, he will never stop.

4. THE BOOR

Boorishness I would define as uncivilized ignorance.

The boor is the sort of man who drinks barley-brew before going into the Assembly; who asserts that garlic smells as sweet as any perfume; wears shoes too big for his feet; and can't talk without bellowing. He won't trust his friends and relations, but he'll consult his slaves about his most important business; and he'll retail all the affairs of the Assembly to the labourers he employs on his farm. He sits down with his clothes hitched above the knee, exposing his nakedness. In the streets, other sights arouse in him no interest or surprise whatever, but if he sees a cow or a donkey or a goat he stops and inspects it. He can't fetch a bit of food from the cupboard without nibbling at it on the way; he drinks his wine neat. He quietly tries to rumple the bakery-maid, after he's helped her to do the grinding for the whole household, himself included. He feeds his horses while still eating his own breakfast. He answers the front door himself; and calls his dog and takes hold of it by the nose, and says, 'This fellow guards the house and the whole place.' When he has been paid by someone with a silver coin, he rejects it, saying it is worn too smooth, and takes another instead. If he has lent his plough, or a basket, or a sickle, or a bag, he remembers it as he lies awake and goes to ask for it in the middle of the night. On his way down to town he asks anyone he meets what price hides or bloaters were fetching, or whether the new-moon festival is being held today. And in the same breath he tells you he's going down to get his hair cut; and while he's passing that way he means to call at Archias's for some fish. He sings in the public bath; and he drives hobnails into his shoes.

5. ANXIETY TO PLEASE

Anxiety to please (to compass it in a definition) is a quality designed to give pleasure, but whose impact does not make the best impression.

The ingratiating man is, shall we say, the sort who greets you from fifty yards off with 'My dear man', gazes at you full of admiration, holds you by both hands and won't let go, and then after accompanying you a little way and asking when he is to see you next, finally departs on a note of eulogy. When he is called in to an arbitration he is anxious to please not only the man he is supporting but also his opponent, so as to appear impartial. In a dispute between foreigners and Athenians he will say the foreigners are in the right. When invited out to dinner he will ask his host to call the children; and when they come in he will say they are as like their father as so many peas in a pod. Then he pulls them towards him, kisses them and makes them stand by him. Then he romps with them, and sings the words of the game himself –

> Atishoo, atishoo,
> We all fall down!

– and he lets some of them fall asleep on his stomach, in spite of the cramp it gives him.

6. THE OUTCAST, OR THE DEMORALIZED MAN

The quality of an outcast is the ready submission to what is degrading, both in act and word.

The demoralized man is one who will take an oath at a moment's notice, being well able to carry a bad name and accept vilification; a man of coarse nature, disreputable habits, and no principles. He is capable, if you will, of dancing the Kordax,[1] sober and without a mask, in a comedy chorus. At street-corner shows he will be the man to go round and collect the coppers, missing no one, and battling with those types who always have a 'pass' and want to see the show for nothing. He is very likely, too, to go in for inn-keeping or brothel-keeping or tax-farming; he shrinks from no disreputable trade – town-crier or hired cook; he gambles, and lets his mother starve; he gets arrested for petty theft, and spends more time in prison than at home.

[2] [In addition, he would seem to be one of those who collect a ring of people, then call up a whole crowd, and carry on abusive arguments in a loud, grating voice; meanwhile some join in the gathering, others wander off before hearing him

1. An obscene dance.   2. This paragraph is probably spurious.

out; some of them get the beginning of his rigmarole, others a resumé, others a fragment; and for making this kind of exhibition he always chooses a time when the town is crowded for some special occasion.]

In the law-courts he is perfectly at home, either conducting his defence, or denying knowledge on oath, or simply appearing with a file of documents tucked into his gown and clusters of memoranda in his hands. It's not beneath him to be a little king among the barrow-boys, lend them money for the asking, and charge twenty-five per cent per day; or to make the rounds of the pie-and-pasty shops, the wet-fishmongers and the dried-fishmongers, and collect the interest due to him straight out of the customer's hand into his mouth[1].

7. THE TALKER

Loquacity, should you want to define it, would seem to be an incontinence of talk.

The talker is the sort of man who, when you meet him, if you make any remark to him, will tell you that you are quite wrong; that he himself knows all the facts, and if you listen to him you shall learn what they are. When you reply, he interrupts you with 'You've already told me, remember, what you're just going to say'; or 'What a good thing you reminded me!' or, 'It's so valuable to have a talk'; or, 'Oh, I just forgot to mention –' or, 'You saw the point at once'; or, 'Yes, I've been watching you to see if you'd come round to my view.' He gives himself openings like this, one after the other, so that you never have time to take breath. Then, when he has talked the hind legs off individual victims, nothing will stop him advancing on groups and gatherings, and making them leave their business in the middle and take to flight. He will even walk into schools or sports-grounds, and hinder boys in their exercises, by talking in this endless way to their

1. A convenient way to carry a coin – as we put a pencil behind the ear.

trainers and teachers. When people say, 'We must go now', he likes to keep them company on the way and see them safely home. When he hears what has happened in the Assembly, he tells you about it; and adds, for good measure, the story of the battle in Aristophon's year, and of the Spartan victory under Lysander; and of the speech he himself once made, which drew some applause from the Assembly; at the same time throwing into his discourse some derogatory remarks about 'the masses'. The result is that his audience either let their attention wander, or drop off to sleep, or desert him in mid-course and vanish. When he is on a jury he prevents his fellow-jurors from reaching a verdict; in a theatre he won't let you follow the play, at a dinner he won't let you eat. 'A talker finds it hard to stop,' he says; and adds that his tongue runs on of itself, and he couldn't stop it, even if people thought him worse than a nest of swallows. He is actually ready to let his own children make fun of him, when they are feeling sleepy and say to him, 'Daddy, talk to us and send us to sleep!'

8. THE INVENTOR OF NEWS

Newsmaking is the fabrication of false reports, which the inventor wants to have believed, about things said and done.

The newsmaker is the kind of man who, on meeting someone, counters his friend's glum look with a smile and asks, 'Where have you come from? and what's your news? Can you give me the latest about this business?' And then, pressing his attack. he asks, 'No new developments? Well, certainly the reports are splendid.' And giving you no chance to reply he goes on, 'What's that? You haven't heard? I can see I'm going to regale you with news.' And he has some soldier, or perhaps a slave of the flute-player Asteios, or it's the contractor Lycon, arrived straight from the battle, from whom he says he has heard all this. In fact, the credentials of his statements are of a kind that no one could possibly check. Quoting his sources, he recounts how Polyperchon and the king have won a battle[1], and Cassandros has been taken prisoner. And if someone asks him, 'Do you believe this?' he will say, 'Why, the whole town's buzzing with it, confirmation keeps coming in, all accounts agree. There's been an almighty mash-up.' For evidence, he says, you have only to look at the faces of men in the Government, and note the change in every one of them. He has heard incidentally, he says, that they have an informant (whom they are keeping hidden) who knows everything. As he unfolds his tale, you will hardly believe how convincingly he moves tears with his 'Poor Cassandros! What a tragic end! Doesn't it make you think – what Chance can do to us? Well, he was a great man once!' And he adds, 'You must be the only one to know this' – when he has already trotted it all round Athens.

[2]What I don't understand about men like this, is why they do it. Not only are they liars, but they show a loss on their day's work. Some of them, as often happens, while holding an audience in the public baths, have had their cloaks stolen; some have lost lawsuits by default while winning victories by land and sea in the Stoa; others, while verbally capturing cities, have missed their dinner. These men's occupation is entirely pitiable; in every public place, in every factory, in every corner of the Agora, they are busy all day long boring their hearers to death and exhausting them with their fabrications.

9. THE SHAMELESS MAN

Shamelessness may be defined as indifference to ill repute for the sake of gain.

The shameless man is one who will go to borrow money from the very person he is defrauding; one who after sacri-

1. See Introduction, page 7.   2. See Introduction, page 9.

ficing to the gods will himself go out to dinner with someone else, and then salt down the meat and store it. At his host's table he calls his slave, then picks up meat and bread from the table and gives it to him, saying so that everyone can hear, 'Make a good meal, Tibeios!' When he goes shopping he reminds the butcher of any little service he may have done him; and he stands near the scale and slips on to it some meat if possible, otherwise a bone to make soup; and if he gets away with it he's happy, and if not, he whips a bit of tripe off the table and chuckles as he hurries away with it. When he has guests from another city he buys (with their money) seats for a theatre performance, and thus sees the play without paying his share; and the next day he even brings his sons, and their tutor. If you are carrying something you've bought at a bargain price, he will always ask you to share it with him. He will go to a neighbour's door and borrow barley, or perhaps bran, and then get the person who has lent it to carry it over to his house. In the public baths, what he likes to do is to go over to where the jugs are kept, fill one (while the bath-man bawls at him), throw water over his own head, and then announce that he has had his bath, adding as he goes out, 'And no thanks to you!'

10. THE SKINFLINT, OR STINGY MAN

Stinginess is a disproportionate avoidance of expense.

The stingy man is the sort who will come to your house in the middle of the month and ask you for half a month's interest on his loan. When he is at table with others, he will count how many cups each person has drunk; and of the whole company at dinner, he will pour the smallest libation to Artemis. If you buy anything for him, however cheaply, he will say, when you send in your account, that it has taken his last penny. If a servant breaks a jug or a dish, he stops the price of it out of his allowance. If his wife has dropped a threepenny-bit, he is the sort of person to start moving the furniture, shifting couches and cupboards, rummaging among rugs. If he has anything to sell, he will only let it go at a price which means a bad bargain for the buyer. He would never let you eat a fig out of his garden, or walk through his land, or pick up one of his windfall olives or dates. Every single day he inspects his boundaries to see if they have been tampered with. He is a terror, too, for enforcing the right of distraint, and for charging compound interest. When it is his turn to give the parish dinner, he cuts the meat into tiny slices to serve out. He goes off to market, and comes home again without buying anything. He forbids his wife to lend salt, or lamp-wick, or herbs, or barley-grains, or garlands, or holy-cakes. 'These things all mount up, you know,' he says, 'in a twelvemonth.'

11. THE ABOMINABLE MAN

Abominable behaviour is not hard to define: it is blatant and offensive levity.

The abominable man is one who on meeting respectable women will lift his clothing and display his private parts. In the theatre he claps when the rest have stopped; and hisses players whom everyone else is enjoying; and when there is a silence he will lift his head and belch, to make the audience turn round. Just when the market is most crowded he goes to the stalls where they sell nuts, or myrtle-berries, or fruit, and stands there nibbling away while he chats to the stall-keeper. In company he will address by name someone with whom he is not acquainted. If he sees that people are in a hurry, he insists on their stopping a little. If you have just lost an important lawsuit he comes up as you leave the court and congratulates you. He goes out to do his own shopping, hires a couple of flute-girls, and then if you meet him shows you what he has got and invites you to come and share them.

He will stand talking outside the barber's or the myrrh-shop, and announce that he intends to get drunk. When his mother has just come in from visiting the fortune-teller he deliberately uses unlucky words. When prayers or libations are going on, he drops his cup and then laughs as if he had done something funny. When he is being played to on the flute, he will be the one person to tap the tune with his fingers and to whistle an accompaniment, and then severely ask the flute-girl why she didn't stop at once. When he wants to spit, he spits across the table at the slave who is pouring wine.

12. THE UNSEASONABLE MAN

Unseasonableness is an annoying faculty for choosing the wrong moment.

The unseasonable man is the kind who comes up to you when you have no time to spare and asks your advice. He sings a serenade to his sweetheart when she has influenza. Just after you have gone bail for somebody and had to pay up, he approaches you with a request that you will go bail for him. If he is going to give evidence he turns up when judgement has just been pronounced. When he is a guest at a wedding he makes derogatory remarks about the female sex. When you have just reached home after a long journey he invites you to come for a stroll. He is certain to bring along a buyer who offers more, when you have just sold your house. When people have heard a matter and know it by heart, he stands up and explains the whole thing from the beginning. He eagerly undertakes a service for you which you don't want performed but which you have not the face to decline. When people are sacrificing and spending money, he arrives to ask for his interest on a loan. When a friend's slave is being beaten he will stand there and tell how he once had a slave who hanged himself after a similar beating. If he takes part in an arbitration, he will set everyone at blows again just when both sides are ready to cry quits. And after dancing once he will seize as partner another man who is not yet drunk.

13. OVERDOING IT

Well, of course, overdoing it will be something like well-meaning presumption in word or act.

The presumptuous man is one who makes the kind of promise he will not be able to keep. When a matter is generally admitted to be just, he raises objections, and is then overruled. He insists on his slave mixing more wine than the company can finish. He tries to separate two men fighting, even when he doesn't know them. He begins to show you a short cut, and presently has no idea where he is going. He will walk up to the colonel and ask him when he intends to put the troops in battle-formation, and what will be his orders for the day after tomorrow. He will go to his father and tell him that his mother is still fast asleep in their bedroom. When the doctor has forbidden an invalid to be given wine, he says he wants to try an experiment, and makes the patient tipsy. When a woman relative has died, he inscribes on her tombstone her husband's name, and her father's and her mother's, as well as her own name and her place of birth, and adds, that 'they were all estimable people'. And when about to take an oath he remarks to those standing round, 'I've done this scores of times.'

14. FECKLESSNESS

Fecklessness, if we are to define it, is slowness of wit in word and action.

The feckless man is one who, after working out some figures on his reckoner, and finding the total, asks the man sitting next to him, 'What does it come to?' When he is defendant in a lawsuit, and the case is due to come on, he forgets and goes off for a day in the country. When he goes to see a play, he gets left behind all alone in the theatre fast asleep. After a heavy supper he gets up in the night to go to the lavatory, and is bitten by his neighbour's dog. He buys something, puts it carefully away himself, and later looks for it and can't find it. When someone informs him that a friend of his has died, so that he can attend the funeral, he says, with a mournful expression and tears in his eyes, 'Well, that's fortunate.' When he receives back money that is owed to him he will insist on having witnesses present. In the middle of winter he has a row with his slave for not buying cucumbers in the market. He compels his own children to wrestle and run even to the point of exhaustion. In the country, if he is going to cook pease-pudding for himself, he puts salt into the pot twice, and makes it uneatable. When it is raining he remarks, 'What a lovely smell from the stars' – when other people would say, 'from the earth'. And when someone asks, 'How many dead bodies do you suppose have been carried out through the Sacred Gate?' he answers with 'I only wish you and I had as many.'

15. THE HOSTILE MAN

Hostility is harshness showing itself in words.

The hostile man is one who, when asked where so-and-so is, replies, 'Don't come bothering me'; or who, when spoken to, will not answer. When he has something to sell, instead of telling the buyers what he will let it go for, he asks them, 'What am I getting for this?' To those who politely send presents when he holds a feast, he says that he wants none of their gifts. If you have accidentally pushed him or trodden on his foot, he never forgives you. When a friend has asked him to contribute a donation, he first says he won't give one; then later he brings it, with the remark, 'More money thrown away.' When he stubs his toe in the road he invariably curses the stone. He can't bear to wait long for anyone. He will never consent to sing, or to recite, or to dance. Probably too he never prays to the gods.

16. THE SUPERSTITIOUS MAN

Ah, yes, superstition: it would appear to be cowardice in face of the supernatural.

The superstitious man is one who, if anything dirty touches him, will wash his hands, sprinkle himself with water from a holy fountain, and walk about all day with his mouth full of bay-leaves. If a weasel crosses his path, he will not go a step further until someone else has overtaken him, or until he has thrown three stones across the road. Should he see a snake in his house, if it's a harmless one he invokes Sabazios; but if it's a venomous one he immediately builds a shrine to Heracles on the very spot. When he passes the smooth stones at a cross-roads he pours oil on them from his flask, and won't leave the place till he has fallen on his knees and kissed them. If a mouse gnaws through a leather bag of barley, off he goes to the expounder of omens and asks what he ought to do. If the reply is that he should take the leather bag to the cobblers and get it patched, he pays no heed to this advice, but turns on his heel and performs an expiatory sacrifice. He likes to purify his house at frequent intervals, saying that something has occurred to attract Hecate. If, when walking, he hears owls hoot, he is alarmed, and will only go on when he has pronounced the words, 'Athene is greater.' He will never set foot on a tomb, or come near a corpse or a woman in childbirth, but says it is important for him to avoid pollution. And on the fours and sevens of the month (i.e., the fourth, seventh, fourteenth, seventeenth, etc.) he instructs his household to put wine on to boil, and goes out and buys myrtle-berries, incense and honey-cakes, and when he comes in again spends the rest of the day putting garlands on the images of Hermaphroditos. When he has had a dream, he is off again to the interpreters, the fortune-tellers, the bird-watchers, to ask which of the gods or goddesses he should pray to. When he is contemplating initiation he visits the Orphic instructors month by month, and takes his wife with him (if she can't spare the time he takes the nurse) and even his children. I should say he will be one of those who meticulously sprinkle themselves with salt water on the sea-shore. And if ever he catches sight of cross-road offerings to Hecate wreathed with garlic, he goes away and washes his head thoroughly, and calls in some wise women and gets them to purify him by walking round him with a lily-bulb or a puppy for sacrifice. If he sees a madman or an epileptic he shivers, and spits into the fold of his gown.

17. A CHIP ON THE SHOULDER, OR THE MAN WITH A GRIEVANCE

To have a 'chip on the shoulder' means to complain unduly about the lot which life has assigned to one.

The man with a grievance is the kind of man who, when a friend has sent him his share of a banquet, remarks to the slave who brings it, 'He doesn't invite me to dinner: that way he saves my share of his soup and his nasty wine.' When his sweetheart is caressing and kissing him he says to her, 'I wonder if you genuinely love me as much as you seem to.' He is resentful against Zeus, not for sending rain, but for sending it too late. If he finds a purse in the road, he says, 'But a fortune – no! I've never found *that*.' When he has bought a slave cheap after much haggling, 'I wonder, now,' says he, 'whether for that money I can have bought anything worth having.' When someone comes to him with the good news, 'You've got a son,' he replies, 'If you add to that, "And away goes half my property," you'll be telling the truth.' When he has won a lawsuit by a unanimous vote, he finds fault with the man who wrote his speech, for omitting a number of strong points. When his friends have contributed to provide him with a loan, and one of them says, 'Now you can feel cheerful,' 'Can I indeed,' he answers, 'when I've got to give every one of you his money back, and on top of that show gratitude, as if I'd been done a favour!'

18. THE DISTRUSTFUL MAN

Lack of trust is the assumption that everyone is cheating you.

The distrustful man is the sort who, after sending a slave to buy provisions, sends another whose job is to find out how much he paid for them. He carries his money himself, and sits down twice in a quarter of a mile to count how much he has. When he's lying in bed he asks his wife if she locked the safe, if the sideboard is sealed, and the front door bolted. If she says Yes, he none the less gets out of bed, naked and barefoot, lights the lamp, and trots round checking everything; and finally with some difficulty gets to sleep again. If you owe him money, he asks for his interest in front of witnesses, to remove all chance of your saying you were not asked for it. He likes to send his coat for cleaning, not to the cleaner who does the best work, but to the one who has a reliable guarantor. When someone comes to borrow silver cups, he refuses if he possibly can; if it is a relative or a close acquaintance, he lends only after taking every precaution short of testing and weighing the metal, or even getting a third party to go bail. When his slave attends him in the street, he orders him to walk in front instead of behind, so that he can keep an eye on him and see that he doesn't run away. If you have bought something from him, and say, 'How much? Put it down to my account, as I haven't time just now to send the money,' he replies, 'Don't put yourself to that trouble; I'll come along with you – until you *have* time.'

19. OFFENSIVENESS

Offensiveness is a neglect of one's personal condition such as to cause annoyance.

The offensive man is one who walks about with eczema or scabs or misshapen finger-nails, and says that he was born with these afflictions; his father and his grandfather, he says, had them just the same – and it's no easy thing to be smuggled into *their* family. And of course it's just like him to have ulcers on the front of his shins, and whitlows on his fingers, and not to look after them but let them fester. He has arm-pits like a bear's, and the hairiness extends across half his body; and his teeth are black and decaying, so that talking with him is thoroughly unpleasant.

Things like this too: he wipes his nose while eating; while engaged in a sacrifice he chews; spits while talking to you; and belches at you in the middle of a drink. He does not wash before getting into bed with his wife. He uses rancid oil in the bath, so that he stinks. He puts on a thick vest and a flimsy cloak covered with stains, and goes off to the market-place like that.

20. THE TIRESOME MAN

Tiresomeness – to attempt a definition – is a quality whose impact causes annoyance rather than actual harm.

The tiresome man is the kind who will walk in when you have just dozed off and wake you up to have a chat with you. When people are on the point of setting sail he will hinder their departure. He will arrive for an appointment, and then ask you to wait till he has taken a walk. He will take his child from its nurse, bite up its food and feed it himself, cooing and clucking at it and calling it 'Daddy's little imp'. When you sit next to him at a meal he will describe to you how he took a dose of hellebore which gave him a thorough clean-out; 'You should have seen the colour of the bile in my excreta,' he says, 'darker than that gravy you've got.' He's a terror for asking his mother, in front of relations, 'Tell me, Mummy, when you were in labour with me, was it an easy birth?' Then he answers for her, and says that childbirth is pleasurable, but that it is not easy to conceive a human being without experiencing both pleasure and pain. He tells you that in his house he has cold water laid on from a reservoir; that he has a garden with many kinds of vegetables, young and tender; that he has a cook who is very clever with fish; that his house is a regular hotel, and his friends are like the proverbial sieve: 'The more you do for them, the less they're satisfied.' When he gives a dinner, he draws his guests' attention to his parasite,[1] commenting on the man's personal qualities. And as he stands over the wine-bowl he announces encouragingly that provision has been made for the pleasure of those present: they have only to ask and his slave will fetch her at once from the agency. 'Then,' he says, 'she will supply us all with music and merriment.'

21. PETTY AMBITION

Petty ambition will be familiar as an undignified craving for marks of respect.

The man of petty ambition is one who, when asked out to dinner, sets great store by sitting next to the host himself during the meal. He takes his son off to Delphi for his ceremonial hair-cut.[2] He takes trouble to have a black slave to attend him in the street. When he returns a loan of one silver mina he makes his slave pay it with a new coin. He has his hair cut very frequently; keeps his teeth white; changes his clothes while they are still good; and uses scented ointment instead of oil. In the Agora he frequents the banking

1. Compare Character 2; and Chaereas in *The Bad-Tempered Man*, page 60.
2. i.e., at his coming of age.

quarter; in the gymnasia he spends his time where the young men are exercising; in the theatre, when there's a performance he chooses a seat near the Strategoi. He buys – for himself, nothing; but all kinds of things for friends abroad; he sends off pickled olives to Byzantium, Spartan hounds to Cyzikos, Hymettos honey to Rhodes; and at the same time lets the whole town know about it. And naturally it's he who must keep a pet monkey, and have a short-tailed ape and some Sicilian doves, and dice made of gazelle-horn, oil-flasks of the round variety from Thurioi, twisted walking-sticks from Sparta, a curtain with a woven design of Persians; and a private wrestling-ground with sand in it, and a hand-ball court. And he goes around lending this place to philosophers, to sophists, to drill-sergeants, to musicians, for giving displays. And when the displays are in progress he himself walks in, rather late, so that spectators turn to each other and say, 'That's the man who owns this place.' Of course he keeps a jackdaw at home; and he must buy a toy ladder for it, and make a tiny bronze shield for the jackdaw to hold while it hops up the ladder. When he has sacrificed an ox, he nails up the forelock, wreathed with enormous garlands, just inside his house opposite the door, so that everyone who comes in can see that he has sacrificed an ox. When he has taken part in a procession of the Knights, he hands all the rest of his equipment to his slave to take home, and then walks about the Agora in his spurs, constantly tossing back his cloak. If his little Maltese terrier has died, he sets up a memorial tablet to it, with the inscription, 'A Scion of Malta'. If he has dedicated a bronze ring in the Temple of Asclepios, he wears it thin with polishing and oiling it every day. And of course he manages to obtain from the Presidents the privilege of announcing to the public the result of a sacrifice. Arrayed in a gleaming cloak, and wearing a wreath, he steps forward and says, 'Athenians! We, the Presidents, have performed the sacrifice of the Galaxia to the Mother of the gods, and the omens are auspicious;

therefore receive her blessing.' After making this proclamation he goes off home and recounts in detail to his wife how exceedingly well everything is going with him.

22. MEANNESS

Meanness is the absence of desire for honour where expense is involved.

The mean man is the sort of person who after winning, as Choregos, first place with his tragedy, then dedicates to Dionysos a wooden tablet, inscribing on it only his own name. When voluntary contributions to public finance are being made in the Assembly, he gets up and quietly slips out. When he is giving his daughter in marriage he sells all the meat of the sacrifice except the portions for the priests, and to attend and serve at the wedding banquet he hires staff who feed at home. When he is trierarch he spreads the helmsman's blankets on the bed for himself, and puts his own blankets away. He has a way of keeping his sons home from school when there is a festival of the Muses, so that they will not have to contribute; and sends a message that they are unwell. When he has been shopping he carries the vegetables from the market himself in a fold of his gown. He stays indoors while his coat is at the cleaner's. If a friend of his is raising a public subscription and has mentioned it to him, should he see him coming he will turn down a side street and go home by a roundabout way. If his wife has brought a dowry, instead of buying a maid for her, he hires from the women's market a slave to attend her when she goes out. He wears shoes that are patched, and says they are as strong as horn. When he gets up he tidies the house and sweeps out the dining-room; and as he sits down he hitches aside the cloak which is the only garment he wears.

23. THE BOASTER

Put plainly, boastfulness would seem to be pretension to advantages which one does not possess.

The boaster is a man who will stand on the jetty talking to foreigners about the vast sums he has at sea; describing the wide extent of his investment in overseas trade, with details of his own gains and losses; and while shooting a great line on this topic, he will send off his boy to the Bank, where his balance is one drachma. If you travel with him, he has you at his mercy; he loves to tell you how he campaigned with Alexander;[1] how he got on with him; how many jewel-encrusted cups he brought home. Then he talks about Asiatic craftsmen, maintaining that they are better than the European; and all this he will say, without having ever travelled outside Attica. He will tell you he has had letters – three in succession – from Antipater[1] inviting him to Macedonia; that he has been offered a licence for tax-free export of timber from Macedonia, but has refused it, so that no one may cast aspersions on him as a pro-Macedonian. In the famine, he says, his outlay in gifts to distressed citizens amounted to more than five talents – 'I never could say No.' Then, though the men sitting next to him are strangers, he tells one of them to work it out in writing; and reckoning in sums of six hundred drachmae or one mina, and speciously assigning a name to each gift, he finally makes it as much as ten talents. He points out that this is the amount contributed by himself to charities, mentioning that it does not include the trierarchies[2] or other public expenses he has undertaken. He will go up to a dealer in horses of quality, and pretend that he wants to buy. He will go into a clothing-store, and ask to see clothing priced at anything up to two talents, and then browbeat his slave for coming without his money. And when he is living in a rented house he will assert,

1. See Introduction, page 7.
2. An undertaking to equip a ship for the navy at one's own expense.

to someone who doesn't know this, that it is the family residence; but he intends to sell it. 'It's a bit small,' he says; 'I do a lot of entertaining.'

24. ARROGANCE

Arrogance is the habit of despising everybody except oneself.

The arrogant man is one who will say, to someone who is in a hurry to speak with him, that he will see him after dinner when he takes his walk. If he has done you a favour, he will mention that he recalls the occasion. If a passer-by asks him to arbitrate a dispute, he gives a quick judgement on the spot. When he is being elected to some public office he declines to stand, stating on oath that he cannot spare the time. He will never make the first approach to anyone. To people who have something to sell, or whom he has employed, he always says, 'Come and see me in the morning.' If he passes you in the street he will not speak to you, but keeps his head bent down, or, when he chooses, looks up in the air. When he entertains friends he does not dine with them himself, but makes one of his servants look after them. When he goes visiting he sends someone ahead to say he is coming. He will allow no one to visit him while he is oiling himself, or washing, or eating. When he is casting an account with someone, you can be sure he will tell his slave to scatter the counters, make a rough total, and book the debt. When sending a business letter, he doesn't write 'I shall be obliged if you will...', but 'I want this done', and 'I wrote expecting to receive...', and 'Make sure my instructions are followed', and 'As quickly as possible'.

25. COWARDICE

Cowardice, let us say, is a sort of shrinking of the soul due to fear.

The coward is the sort of man who, when at sea, is sure that the cliffs just sighted are pirate vessels; or on meeting a heavy swell, asks if there is any uninitiated person on board; or looks up at the steersman to ask if he is on mid-course, or what he thinks of the weather; and explains to the man next to him that his fear is due to a dream he had; and takes off his tunic and gives it to his slave, and begs him to help him to the shore. On military service, when the infantry are marching out to battle, he calls his fellow-townsmen and tells them to stand near him and have a look round first, and remarks that it's a job to tell which lot are the enemy. Then when he hears shouting and sees men falling, he tells those standing next to him that in his hurry he forgot his sword; and he runs back to the tent, and sends his slave out, telling him to look and see where the enemy are; and meanwhile he hides his sword under his pillow, and then spends a long time looking for it; and while he's in the tent he sees a wounded man being brought in – one of his friends; so he runs to him, tells him to cheer up, and lends a hand to carry him. Then he looks after him, washes him, sits down beside him, and flicks the flies off his wound – in fact, anything rather than fight the enemy. When the trumpet sounds the advance, he remains sitting in the tent, and says, 'To hell with you! Can't you let the man get a bit of sleep – always blaring away!' Then, covered with blood from the other man's wound, he meets the men as they come back from the battle, and recounts how – at some risk to himself – he has 'saved one of our comrades'; and he brings the men of his tribe in to see the patient, and describes to each of them how with his own hands he brought the man back to the tent.

26. THE AUTHORITARIAN

Authoritarianism, or the oligarchic temperament, may be described as an arrogant relish for power and profit.

The authoritarian is the sort of person who, when the Assembly is discussing what men to appoint as assistants to the

Archon in organizing the procession at the Great Dionysia, will come forward and state his opinion that those appointed should be given unconditional powers; and if someone else proposes ten assistants, he will answer, 'One is enough, but he must be a *man*.' Of the poems of Homer there is one single line he has made his own:

From many rulers no good comes; let one man rule.

Of all the rest of Homer he knows nothing. Typical of him are utterances like this: 'We must get together by ourselves and discuss these matters, out of reach of the rabble and the street-corner. It's time we stopped kow-towing to every jack-in-office, and ourselves accepting kicks or compliments from them. Either they or we must run this city.' He will go out about midday, with his cloak thrown well back, his hair taste-fully trimmed, his nails precisely pared, and strut about de-claiming statements like this: 'These blackmailers make Athens impossible to live in'; or, 'In the law-courts we are simply slapped down by corrupt juries'; or, 'People who meddle in politics – I can't imagine what they want'; or, 'The working classes – they're always the same: ungrateful, and ready to obey anyone who offers a bribe or a bonus.' Or he will tell you how ashamed he feels in the Assembly, when some mean-looking, scruffy citizen sits down next to him. 'The rich are being bled to death,' he says, 'with subsidizing the navy, the theatre, the festivals, and everything else. When is it going to end? Democratic agitators – how I detest them!' Then he names Theseus as the original cause of the country's deterioration; for it was he who concentrated the twelve small States in one, thus elevating the lower classes, putting power into the hands of the majority, and destroying the monarchy. He adds that Theseus got his deserts; for he was himself the first victim of democracy. And many other such assertions he bestows on foreigners and on Athenians whose temperament and policies are similar to his.

27. LATE LEARNING

Late learning would seem to be a love of difficult tasks which is excessive in view of one's age.

The late learner is the sort of man who, at sixty, learns by heart speeches from the tragedies, and when reciting them over the wine forgets them. He gets his son to instruct him how to do a 'right wheel' or 'left wheel' or 'about turn'. At heroes' festivals he competes with boys in the torch-race. And of course, if he is invited somewhere to a feast of Heracles and asked to choose a victim, he throws off his cloak and chooses the bull, so that he can bend back its neck for slaughter. He goes into the wrestling-schools and submits to training. At a variety show he will sit through three or four performances, learning the songs by heart. When undergoing initiation in the mysteries of Sabazios, he is determined to acquit himself the best in the eyes of the priest. He falls in love with a girl of the town, and when caught by a rival client in the act of forcing her door with a crowbar, and given a beating, he then brings an action for assault. He rides out to the country on a borrowed horse, practises horsemanship on the way, falls off, and breaks his head. At a tenth-day festival he collects a group to sing with him. He plays at 'Long John' with his own slave. He competes at archery and javelin-throwing with his children's tutor, whom he advises to learn from *him* – as if the tutor too knew nothing about it. When wrestling at the baths he wriggles his bottom rapidly, so that people may think he has been properly trained; and when there's a performance of women's dancing, he too practises the steps, whistling the tune for himself.

28. THE SLANDERER

The habit of slander is a bias of the mind towards evil-speaking.

The slanderer is the sort of man who, when asked who so-

and-so is, replies, 'Well, then, shall I begin, like the genealogists, with his parentage? His father was a man who was originally called Sosias; in the army he was known as Sosistratos; and on being enrolled in his deme changed to Sosidemos. His mother is a nobly-born lady of Thrace – at least she answers to the name of "Sweetie"; and I'm told that ladies of that kind are regarded as noble in their own country. The man himself – as you would expect from his antecedents – is a bad lot – a thorough jail-bird.' Or he will say to someone in a nasty tone, 'Oh, I know that kind of trash well enough, that you've come all this way to plead for.' Then he goes on to give details: 'These women grab men out of the street as they pass the door'; or, 'In that house you'll always find them with their feet up. Oh, it's not such nonsense as you might think; why, the women couple in the street like dogs.' Or, 'They talk nothing but men'; or, 'They sit just inside the front door, listening for callers.' Then if other people are talking slander, naturally he'll join in with, 'Yes, I hate him too, more than anyone. You can tell from his face he's a criminal. His wickedness is unique – I'll give you an instance. His wife brought him a good dowry – several talents; she has given him a son; yet her allowance for sweets is three-halfpence, and he makes her wash in cold water in mid-winter.' If he's sitting next to you he always makes remarks about anyone who has just left; and once he has begun, he will not stop short of abusing even his relations. In fact he will utter all manner of slander against friends, relations, even against the dead. And he miscalls his behaviour 'plain speaking' or 'democratic freedom', and makes it his chief pleasure in life.

29. LOVE OF EVIL

By 'love of evil' I mean a partiality for the criminal character.

The 'lover of evil' is the sort of man who contacts those

who have lost lawsuits or been found guilty in criminal cases, and reckons that by associating with them he will become more experienced and more formidable. If someone is referred to as honest, he adds, 'To all appearance', and goes on to say that there is no such thing as an honest man; that all men are alike; indeed he uses the phrase 'What a good man' as a joke. A criminal type he will describe as 'Independent-minded, if you look at him fairly. Many of the things people say of him,' he admits, 'are true; but there are some things they don't know. He's naturally talented; he sticks to his friends; and he's no fool.' He insists emphatically that he has never met a more capable person. He will take the side of a man who is making his defence in the Assembly, or on trial in a law-court; and he will probably tell the jury that 'They must judge the case and not the man.' He will describe the defendant as a 'watchdog of the people, one who keeps his eye on wrong-doers. Unless we value such men,' he says, 'we shall have no one left who cares what goes wrong in public life.' He can't resist championing worthless men; on a jury he organizes a pressure-group in a bad cause; when judging a case he takes the statements of the opposed parties in the worst sense.

30. THE AVARICIOUS MAN

Avarice is the craving for sordid gain.

The avaricious man is one who when giving a party will not put out enough bread for his guests. He borrows from a man of another city who is spending a night with him. When distributing shares at a club feast, he says it is right that a double share should be given to the distributor – and immediately helps himself. When he has wine for sale, he sells it to his friend watered. If he travels on a public commission, he leaves at home the money provided by the State for his expenses, and borrows from his fellow-deputies; he loads his servant with a heavier pack than he can carry, and gives him smaller rations than anyone else in the group; and if any presents are given by their hosts, he demands his full share – and sells it. When he is anointing himself at the baths, he says to his slave, 'Here, this oil you've bought is rancid,' and uses someone else's. If his slaves find a bag of coppers in the street, he cries out, 'Luck's for all,' and claims his share. He sends his cloak to the cleaner's, borrows another from an acquaintance, and trails it round for days afterwards, till the owner has to ask for it back.

Other little ways of his are: he measures out the rations for his household with his own hands, using a 'thrifty' can with the bottom knocked in, and brushing off the top very close. He beats down a friend who thinks he is selling something reasonably, and once he has got it, goes and sells it. And you may be sure, when he is paying a debt of thirty minas, that he will pay it four drachmas short. If his sons have missed some days from school through illness, he deducts from the month's fee a proportionate sum; and during the month Anthesterion, because there are so many festival days, he saves the fee by not sending them to their lessons at all. When he has hired out his slave, and is receiving from him the money due, he asks for the discount as well; and when holding an audit he makes the same demand from the administrator under question. When entertaining the men of his clan, he begs a dish from the common table for his own slaves; and he makes a list of the half-radishes that are left over, so that the waiters won't get them. When he is travelling with a party of acquaintances, he uses their slaves, lets his own slaves out on hire, and does not contribute the hire-money to the common fund. When his club meets at his house for dinner, it is just like him to put aside for himself a portion of the provisions contributed, such as firewood, lentils, vinegar, salt, or lamp-oil. If a friend, or a friend's daughter, is getting married, some time before the wedding he goes travelling abroad, to avoid sending a present. And the things he borrows from acquaintances are the kind of things one would never ask to have back, or would hardly accept even if they were offered.

THE SPURIOUS PREFACE[1]

My dear Polycles,

I have often wondered, when I have given the matter thought – and it may be I shall never stop wondering – why it is that we Greeks, living as we do in a country with a uniform climate and all receiving the same education, don't all happen to have the same character. I have studied human nature for a long time, and am now ninety-nine years old; moreover, I have mixed with many people of all nationalities and have very closely compared good characters with bad; and therefore I felt it was my duty to write down the different habits of life displayed by both kinds. I shall set before you, one by one, all the various types into which men are divided, and show how they manage their affairs. For I believe, my dear Polycles, that our sons will be the better men for having had bequeathed to them such object-lessons, which they may study as examples, and which will teach them to choose the company and conversation of the men of highest principles, and to endeavour not to fall below their level. Now I will turn to my theme; and it is for you to follow my argument and judge if I am right. I will dispense with prelude and preamble; and I will begin with Irony and those who make irony their aim. I will define it, and then I will describe the ironical man, showing the sort of person he is, and the sort of life his nature makes him lead; and then I will try to illustrate other conditions one by one, as I have set out to do.

1. See Introduction, page 8.

Menander

DYSKOLOS

OR

THE BAD-TEMPERED MAN

CHARACTERS

PAN, *the god of country life*
SOSTRATOS, *a rich young man from town*
CHAEREAS, *his parasite*
PYRRHIAS, *a young slave of Sostratos*
CNEMON, *a bad-tempered old farmer*
MYRRHINE, *his daughter*
DAOS, *an old slave of Gorgias*
GORGIAS, *Myrrhine's half-brother*
SICON, *a hired cook*
CALLIPPIDES, *Sostratos' father*
GETAS, *his slave*
SIMICE, *an old woman, slave of Cnemon, and Myrrhine's nurse*
Sostratos' mother and sister; Gorgias' mother; various guests

*

Scene: Phyle in Attica. In the centre of the stage is the entrance to a rustic shrine. On the right is Cnemon's house, on the left Gorgias'. By the entrance to the shrine is a statue of Pan.

SCENE ONE

Enter PAN *from the shrine.*

PAN: Imagine that this place is Phyle in Attica;
  That this cave from which I have come is a shrine of the
    Nymphs,
  A well-known holy place belonging to the people of Phyle—
  Those of them who manage to cultivate these rocks.
  This farm on my right is the home of Cnemon, an old man
  Who prefers his own to anyone else's company;
  Surly-tempered to everybody; detests crowds.
  Crowds, did I say? He has never yet in all his life –
  And that's a good many years – uttered a pleasant word
  To a single soul; never opened a conversation;
  Except that, being my neighbour, he will speak in passing
  To me, Pan, because he's obliged to; but I'm sure
  A moment later he wishes he hadn't.
                       Yet this man,
  This surly creature, married a widow, whose first husband
  Had newly died, leaving her with one little boy.
  Joined to her in the state of holy acrimony
  He spent his days, and a great part of his nights as well,
  In quarrelling – an unhappy life. When a girl was born
  Things became worse; until at last they reached a point
  Where misery beggared all comparison, and the woman,
  Finding her life intolerable, left him and went back
  To live with her son by her first marriage, Gorgias.
  He, now grown up, has this little farm next door, where he
    keeps
  His mother and one faithful slave who belonged to his father.
  They are poor; but the lad has common sense beyond his
    years;
  For hard experience quickly matures a man.

Old Cnemon, with his daughter, and an aged crone
To serve them, lives a lonely life, fetching in logs,
Digging, toiling away; and loathing every soul
Without exception, from his own wife and his neighbours
   here
To the villagers of Cholargos further down the valley.
But the girl does honour to her simple upbringing;
She is pure, good-hearted; serves with devoted piety
The Nymphs, who are my companions. So she inspires in
   us
A wish to help her.
                  Not far from here a wealthy man
Farms an estate worth many talents. This man's son,
A town-bred youth, happened to come here with a friend
Hunting. He saw Cnemon's daughter. I made him fall
Madly in love. So that's the outline of the plot;
The details you can hear if you choose – and please do
   choose!
I think I see him coming, this lover – and his friend,
Both deep in conversation about this very thing.

       [*Exit* PAN. *Enter* SOSTRATOS *and* CHAEREAS.]

CHAEREAS: What was it you said, Sostratos? You saw a girl,
   A free-born girl here, bringing garlands for the Nymphs,
   And you fell in love at once?

SOSTRATOS: At once.

CHAEREAS: Fast work. Surely
   You'd made your mind up, when you first set out from
   home,
   To fall in love with someone?

SOSTRATOS: You laugh, Chaereas;
   But I'm in a bad way.

CHAEREAS: I believe you.

SOSTRATOS: And that's why
   I've brought you here to help me. You're my friend, I'm
   sure;

And you always know what to do.

CHAEREAS: In such matters, Sostratos,
This is the way I go to work. Say, one of my friends
Is keen on a girl, asks me to help. If she's one of that sort,
I act in a flash – I simply allow no argument;
I get drunk, burn her door down, swoop and carry her off.
Before I even ask who she is, she must be had.
The longer he waits, you see, the more he falls in love;
While if he enjoys her soon he soon gets over it.
But if it's marriage he talks of, with a free-born girl,
I take a different line; enquire about her family,
Her life, the sort of girl she is; for in this case
I leave my friend a souvenir for the rest of his life
Of my own efficiency in these matters.

SOSTRATOS: Excellent –
[aside] But not exactly what I wanted.

CHAEREAS: Now I must hear
The whole story.

SOSTRATOS: You know Pyrrhias, the boy who hunts
with us?

CHAEREAS: Yes.

SOSTRATOS: Well, early this morning I sent him off with a
message.

CHAEREAS: A message – yes, who for?

SOSTRATOS: I told him to see her father,
Or whatever man's in charge of the house –

CHAEREAS: Oh, Heracles!
You didn't do *that*?

SOSTRATOS: It was a mistake. It's hardly the thing
To send a *slave* on such a business. When you're in love
It isn't easy to know what's best. I wonder, now,
What can have kept Pyrrhias all this time. I told him
To find out how the land lay there, and come straight
back.

[Enter PYRRHIAS, *running and breathless.*]

PYRRHIAS: Look out! Get away quick, everyone clear out!
   He's mad,
   There's a madman after me.

SOSTRATOS: What's all this?

PYRRHIAS: Get out of his way!

SOSTRATOS: Whose way?

PYRRHIAS: I'm being pelted with sods and rocks. I'm
   wrecked.

SOSTRATOS: Who's pelting you? – Here, where are you off to?
         [SOSTRATOS *seizes* PYRRHIAS, *who thus has time to*
         look round and see that he is not being pursued.]

PYRRHIAS: Perhaps he isn't
   Chasing me any longer.

SOSTRATOS: He isn't.

PYRRHIAS [*mopping his brow*]:   I thought he was.

SOSTRATOS: What *are* you talking about?

PYRRHIAS [*nervously*]:   Look here, now – let's get away.

SOSTRATOS: Where to?

PYRRHIAS: Away from that door, as far as possible.
   He's a son of mischief, the devil's in him, he's lunatic –
   The man who lives there, in that house you sent me to.
   The brute! O gods, my toes! I've pretty near broken them
   all
   On these rocks.

SOSTRATOS: Chaereas, he must have been rude to the man.

PYRRHIAS: I'm sure he's coming back here to set on me again.
   By Zeus, I tell you, Sostratos, we'll all be murdered.

SOSTRATOS: You won't be murdered. Now just tell me
   carefully
   Exactly what you said when you spoke to him.

PYRRHIAS: I can't.
   I'm shaking, and I'm out of breath.

SOSTRATOS [*getting hold of him*]:   You'll tell me now.

PYRRHIAS: Well, first I knocked at the door, and said I
   wished to see

The master. A wretched hag came out, and stood over there,
Where I was talking just now, and pointed him out to me
Up on that hillside, prowling round his blasted pear-trees
Collecting wood enough for a gallows made to measure.

SOSTRATOS: How terrifying! Go on, go on.

PYRRHIAS: Well, then I went
Into the field and walked towards him. And I thought
I'd show him I was a really friendly, capable sort
Of chap; so I called out to him – still quite a long way off –
'I've come to see you on urgent business, sir,' I said,
'Of moment to yourself, sir,' I said. 'Damn you,' says he,
'Who told you to walk into my field?' With that he picks
    up
A lump of turf and slings it slap into my face.

CHAEREAS: Hell! To the crows with him!

PYRRHIAS: And as I blinked, and yelled
'Poseidon drown you!' he picked up a stick this time, and
    beat me
With it, and bellowed, 'What business have you got with
    me?'
At the top of his voice, and, 'Don't you know the public
    road?'

CHAEREAS [to Sostratos]: This farmer friend of yours is a
    plain lunatic.

PYRRHIAS: In the finish, I ran. He chased me best part of two
    miles,
Right round the hill, then down here through the thorn-
    bushes,
Pelting me first with sods and stones, then with his pears
When he hadn't anything else. He's a proper old savage,
A holy terror. Come away, plea . . . se!

SOSTRATOS: I'm not afraid of him.

PYRRHIAS: You don't know what a beast he is. He'll eat us
    raw.

CHAEREAS: Perhaps he's feeling a bit upset today. I think

You might do well to put off meeting him, Sostratos.
There's always a right time for everything; and that's
A good practical rule, you take my word for it.

PYRRHIAS [*fervently*]: You're so right.

CHAEREAS: Penniless peasants are almost all like that –
Vicious tempered; he's not the only one. Tomorrow,
First thing, I'll come here alone, now that I know the house,
And talk to him. Now I'm off home; you go home, too,
And wait a bit, see? Everything's going to be all right.
          [*Exit* CHAEREAS.]

PYRRHIAS: Yes, let's go home.

SOSTRATOS: Ha! Chaereas jumped at the excuse.
It was obvious he disliked coming here with me,
And disapproved my plan to marry. As for you, Pyrrhias,
You wretch, may all the gods blast you as you deserve!

PYRRHIAS: What, *me*? What have *I* done, Sostratos? Eh?
    What have I done?
I didn't do any damage in the man's field, or steal –
Not a single thing.

SOSTRATOS: No? So the man was beating you
For doing nothing?

PYRRHIAS: Look! He's coming! That's the man!
I'm going, I am, sir! You talk to him yourself.
          [*Exit* PYRRHIAS.]

SOSTRATOS: Oh, but I can't. I never make a good impression
When I start talking. What do you *say* to a man like this?
He certainly looks anything but kind. By Zeus,
What a rage he's in! Here, I'll stand back from the door a
    bit –
That's better. Why, as he walks he's mumbling to himself.
He doesn't look sane to me. Apollo and all the gods!
I'm frightened – that's the truth, I may as well confess it.
          [*Enter* CNEMON.]

CNEMON: Now Perseus was a famous man. What luck he had!
First, he had wings – could fly about in the air. That meant

He never had to meet a soul that walks on earth.
Second, he had an invaluable possession, with which
He could turn everyone who annoyed him into stone.
If only I had that power now! There'd be nothing
More plentiful anywhere than fine stone statues.
As it is – by Asclepios, life grows impossible.
People come trespassing on my ground and chat to me.
I've taken to spending my days on the public highway,
    have I?
Why, I don't even *work* this bit of land any more,
I've given it up, to avoid the people who pass by;
And now – they hunt me up to the hill-tops. Curse them all,
There are too many *people*! – Oh, for pity's sake, there's
    another,
Standing at my front door!

SOSTRATOS: Is he going to hit me now?

CNEMON: Where can one get away from *people*? Even if a man
    Wanted to hang himself he couldn't do it in private.

SOSTRATOS: It's me he's angry with. – Excuse me, sir, I'm
    waiting
For someone here; I've made an appointment.

CNEMON [*choking with rage*]:   Didn't I say so?
    Do you take this for a public square or a market-place?
        [*He advances on* SOSTRATOS, *who retreats.*]
    Go on, then! If there's anyone you want to see,
    Come to my door – why not? Do all your business here!
    While you're about it, bring your favourite arm-chair!
    Build a committee-room, just here at my front door!
        [*He leaves* SOSTRATOS *and turns back to his house.*]
    Sheer, shouting rudeness – that's the trouble nowadays.
        [*Exit* CNEMON *to his house.* PYRRHIAS *creeps back,
        but keeps out of Sostratos' way.*]

SOSTRATOS: It seems I've taken on no ordinary job;
    This plainly calls for special measures. Should I go
    And fetch my father's slave Getas? By God, I will.

There's a spark about him; and he's seen a lot of the world.
Let the old man rave – Getas will be a match for him.
I don't believe in wasting time; a lot can happen
In one day. – Why, here's someone coming out of his house.
            [*Enter* MYRRHINE *from Cnemon's house.*]

MYRRHINE: Oh, what shall I do now? Isn't that just my luck?
Nurse dropped the bucket down the well!

SOSTRATOS: O Father Zeus!
Saviour Apollo, and Heavenly Twins! What loveliness!
She's ravishing!

MYRRHINE: Father told us when he left the house
To get hot water ready.

SOSTRATOS [*appealing to audience*]: Athenians! Did you
    ever . . . ?

MYRRHINE: If he finds out, he'll beat her terribly. Oh, dear!
By the two goddesses, there's not a moment to lose –
            [*She turns towards the shrine, hesitating.*]
Dear Nymphs, I'll have to take some water from your spring.
            [*She sees Sostratos.*]
There's someone in there making an offering. I daren't
Disturb him.

SOSTRATOS: Please, give *me* your jug; I'll dip it in
And bring it to you.

MYRRHINE [*handing him the jug*]: Will you? Very well, please
    do.

SOSTRATOS [*aside*]: What charm, what breeding! – and a
    country girl!

MYRRHINE [*turning suddenly round*]:   Oh, gods!
What sound was that? Is it father coming? How terrible!
He'll beat me if he finds me here.
            [*The door of the house on the left opens and* DAOS *comes
            out.* MYRRHINE, *relieved, turns to the shrine to look
            for Sostratos.*]

DAOS [*speaking back into the house, addressing Gorgias' mother
    inside*]:   Now look: I know

66

That you're my mistress; but I've stayed in long enough
Doing chores for you, while your son Gorgias is out
In the field digging, single-handed. I'm going to help him.
>   [*He slams the door.*]
Oh, hateful, damnable Poverty, why did we get
So large a share of you? Why have you come to stay
So many years in our house, a guest who never leaves?

SOSTRATOS [*to Myrrhine*]: Here's your jug. Come nearer,
>   take it.
>   [MYRRHINE *takes it and goes towards her door.*]

DAOS [*looking from one to the other*]: What's *he* doing there?

SOSTRATOS [*to Myrrhine*]: Good-bye now, and attend to your
>   father.
>   [*Exit* MYRRHINE.]
>   Oh, she's gone,
And I'm in misery.
>   [PYRRHIAS *comes forward.*]

PYRRHIAS: Now stop moaning, Sostratos.

SOSTRATOS: Oh, *you*'ve come back.

PYRRHIAS: Everything'll turn out all right.

SOSTRATOS: Turn out all right? How?

PYRRHIAS: Never worry. Simply do
What you were going to do: find Getas, and explain
The whole thing to him clearly; and then come back
>   here.
>   [*Exeunt* SOSTRATOS *and* PYRRHIAS *together.*]

DAOS: Now, what the mischief? I don't like the look of this.
A young man making up to Myrrhine? Most improper.
Cnemon, may the gods punish you for the fool you are!
This innocent girl – instead of keeping guard on her,
You leave her alone out here, with no one else about.
This fellow, I'll bet, as soon as he heard the coast was clear,
Blessed his good luck, and flew straight to her. Well, I'd best
Tell Gorgias immediately what's going on;
Then we can both keep a more careful eye on her.

I think I'll go and talk to him now.
    [*Voices are heard approaching, talking and singing.*]
                  There are people coming,
With offerings for Pan. They've had a drop to drink;
This is no time to get involved with *them*. I'm off.
    [*Exit* DAOS.]

FIRST CHORAL INTERLUDE

SCENE TWO

GORGIAS *and* DAOS *come from the field.*

GORGIAS: And you mean to say you dealt with such a situation
  In this off-handed, feeble manner?
DAOS: What do you mean?
GORGIAS: I mean, by Zeus, when you saw this fellow go up
  to her,
  You ought to have thrown him out on the spot, whoever
  he is,
  And warned him not to let anyone catch him at it again;
  Not stand aside as if it were no concern of yours.
  You've duties to our family, Daos, that you can't shirk.
  Myrrhine's still my sister, and I'm concerned for her.
  I know her father wants to have nothing to do with us;
  But why should we copy his ill nature? If Myrrhine finds
  Herself in trouble, *I'm* going to be blamed as well.
  Neighbours don't know whose fault it is; they see what's
  happened
  To the girl, and nothing else.
DAOS: I tell you, Gorgias,
  The old man frightens me. The moment he sees me coming
  Anywhere near his door, he shouts, 'I'll have you whipped!'
GORGIAS: Yes, you'll find him an awkward customer to argue
  with.
  Nobody knows how to *compel* him to reform;
  Nobody can give him advice or win him over.
  He's got the law on his side – so he can't be compelled;
  And he's got a devil in him – so he won't be advised.
DAOS: But soft – what have we here?[1] We're in the nick of
  time –
  I said he'd soon be back.

---

  1. This line in Greek has a distinctly conventional rhythm, suggesting the
style of tragedy.

GORGIAS: Is that him in the fancy cloak?

DAOS: That's him.

GORGIAS: He's up to no good, you can tell that at
one glance.

[*Enter* SOSTRATOS *with* PYRRHIAS.]

SOSTRATOS: I couldn't get hold of Getas, he was out. My
mother
Is going to hold a sacrifice to some god or other
And she's asked her friends. Oh, yes, she does that every day –
Tours the whole district celebrating sacrifices;
And she's sent Getas out to hire a cook. So I
Said, 'To hell with the sacrifice,' and came back here.
I've had enough of this roundabout way of doing things;
I'll talk to the man myself. I'll knock at his door, before
I've time to consider it further.

GORGIAS: Would you mind, young man,
Listening a moment to something important I have to say?

SOSTRATOS: Certainly. What is it?

GORGIAS: I believe that everyone,
Rich or poor, comes to a point where his luck will end,
And a change set in. The successful man, I believe, will find
His affairs continue to prosper just so long as he
Can carry his luck without doing wrong to anyone.
But, once his good luck leads him to do wrong, why then
He'll meet a change for the worse. And so with poor men
too:
If they are not led by poverty into wrong-doing,
But bear their bad luck bravely, they may hope, with time,
To come to the end of trouble and see happier days.
You take my meaning, then? Don't, just because you're rich,
Rely too much on that; and don't look down on us
Because we're poor. Let people see, by what you do,
That you deserve to keep your good luck all your life.

SOSTRATOS: And what crime do you imagine I'm committing
now?

GORGIAS: I'd say you'd set your mind on doing a rotten thing:
　You want to tempt a free-born girl to her disgrace,
　Watching your chance to do a thing that you'd deserve
　To die for ten times over.

SOSTRATOS:　　　　　　Well, I'm . . . !

GORGIAS:　　　　　　　　　　　It's not fair,
　When *you*'ve got leisure, and *we* haven't, you should use it
　To injure us. When a poor man feels an injury,
　Remember this, there's no one can turn nastier.
　First he feels sorry for himself; but soon he takes
　The wrong he's suffered for insult more than injury.

SOSTRATOS: Now, lad, as you hope for luck, just listen –

PYRRHIAS:　　　　　　　　　　Bravo, master!

SOSTRATOS: I tell you I wish you every kind of luck. You've had
　Your say; now let *me* talk a little. I saw a girl
　Who lives here. I'm in love with her. So, if *this* is
　The injury you speak of, I suppose I'm guilty.
　What should I say? I've come here now not to meet *her*,
　But to see her father. I'm a free man, pretty well off;
　But I'm ready to take her without a dowry, and give my
　　oath
　To love her faithfully. If I came here to do any wrong,
　Or scheming anything underhand against any of you,
　May this god Pan, and all the Nymphs as well, my friend,
　Strike me helpless, here and now in front of your house.
　I tell you it upsets me deeply that you should think
　I was that sort of fellow.

GORGIAS:　　　　　　If I spoke too strongly,
　Please don't let it upset you any more. You have
　Convinced me I was wrong; what's more, you can count
　　on me
　As a friend – and when I say that, bless you, I have the right:
　I'm Myrrhine's half-brother; and from now on, by Zeus,
　I can be of help to you.

SOSTRATOS: What sort of help?

GORGIAS: Listen –
I see you're a good-hearted fellow. I don't want
To disappoint you with empty promises; instead,
I'll tell you plainly how things are. Myrrhine's father –
There's never been another like him, past or present.

SOSTRATOS: You mean old Sour-guts? Yes, I've had a taste
of him.

GORGIAS: It's a very difficult situation. He owns this farm,
Which is worth perhaps two talents; and year in year out
He works the place alone – won't have a soul to help.
He keeps not a single man in the house; he won't employ
A local farm-hand; even neighbours can't get near;
He does the lot himself. His greatest pleasure is
To see no one at all. Most of the time he keeps
His daughter by him as he works. He talks to her,
And it's hard work to make him talk to anyone else.
She shall marry, he says, when he finds a husband for her
who's
Another one like himself.

SOSTRATOS: Well, that means never.

GORGIAS: My friend,
Don't take the job on; you'll get nowhere. He's *our* burden,
As luck would have it – we're his family.

SOSTRATOS: Good gods!
Lad, have you never been in love?

GORGIAS: No, friend, I can't
Afford it.

SOSTRATOS: Why? What stops you?

GORGIAS: Simple arithmetic.
Adding up bad luck leaves no time for falling in love.

SOSTRATOS: So I gather: you talk like a man who knows
nothing about it.
You say, 'Give it up' – but I no longer have any choice:
The god has chosen for me. [*He points to the statue of* PAN.]

GORGIAS: Well, you do *us* no harm;
You simply go through misery and get nothing for it.

SOSTRATOS: What if I win the girl?

GORGIAS: You won't win her. – Unless,
Perhaps – I'm going up to the hill – you could come too
And stand beside me; *he* works the next field to ours.

SOSTRATOS: How would that help?

GORGIAS: I'll drop a casual word to him
About his daughter getting married. That's a thing
I'd be very glad to see –

DAOS: You try: he'll start a war
Straight off on everyone, hurling insults at the way
His neighbours live. [*To Sostratos*] And if he sees *you* idling
there
Keeping your hands clean, he'll not stand the sight of you.

SOSTRATOS: Is he there now?

GORGIAS: Not now, but in a little while
He'll go out by his usual way.

SOSTRATOS: Do you say he takes
Myrrhine with him? My dear man, for the chance of that
I'll gladly come as you suggest. I beg you, now,
Throw all your weight in on my side.

DAOS [*sourly*]: Just how do you mean?

SOSTRATOS: How? [*To Gorgias*] Come on, let's be going as
you said.

DAOS: Now look:
We're going to work. Are you going to stand next to us
Wearing that fancy cloak?

SOSTRATOS: Why not?

DAOS: He'll pick up clods
And throw them at you, and call you a lazy pest. You've got
To dig along with us. If he saw you doing that
Who knows but he might condescend to hear a word
Even from you, if he thought you were a poor farm-hand
Earning your living.

SOSTRATOS: I'll do anything you say. Lead on.

GORGIAS [aside to Daos]: Why are you forcing him to go through agony?

DAOS [aside to Gorgias]: I tell you what: we'll do the heaviest day's work
You ever saw, and make the young fool rupture himself.
That'll stop him coming around and getting in our way.

SOSTRATOS: Fetch me a hoe.[1]

DAOS: You'd better take mine. I'll spend the time
Mending the wall – that's got to be done too.

SOSTRATOS: Give it me.

DAOS [aside to Sostratos]: You've saved my life. [To Gorgias]
I'm going down to the wall, master;
You'll find me there.
[Exit DAOS.]

SOSTRATOS: My mind's made up: either I die
Now, or I win Myrrhine and live.

GORGIAS: If what you say
Is what you really mean, why then I wish you luck.

SOSTRATOS: By the holy gods! Every discouragement *you*
think
Will stop me, doubles my resolution to go on.
[Exit GORGIAS.]
– She's a girl who wasn't brought up in a crowd of women;
She knows nothing of the sins and sorrows of this life,
Was never frightened by any aunt or nurse; she has lived
With this old father of hers – he's a bit rough, but gives her
A free-born home, and hates bad characters. Well, then,
Surely to win this girl would be a wonderful thing? . . .
This hoe weighs half a ton, it'll kill me. All the same
No weakening now! I've begun – I must go through with it.
[Exit SOSTRATOS *following Gorgias to the field.*
SICON *the cook enters dragging a sheep by a rope.*]

1. This hoe was a two-pronged tool apparently used for a variety of pur-
poses – as will appear later.

SICON: This ruddy sheep's enough to break your ruddy heart.
Ah, go to hell! If I pick it up and carry it,
It gets its teeth on the branch of a tree and chews the leaves
And tears the branch off. Same if I put it down on the ground,
It won't get moving. Talk about slaughter! – it's not the sheep,
It's me, the cook, gets slaughtered, dragging this battleship.
Well, gods above be praised, here's the shrine of the Nymphs,
Where the banquet is. My greetings to great Pan!

[GETAS *appears from the direction of the town, carrying a bundle of cushions.*]

Here, Getas!
What sort of time is this to arrive?

GETAS: Those damned women –
Look at the load they strapped on me: enough to break
Four donkeys.

SICON: Seems there must be a lot of people coming –
That's an enormous bundle of cushions you've got there.

GETAS: Cushions? What haven't I got?

SICON: Pile them up here.

GETAS: There. Whew!
You know that Pan at Paeania, fifteen miles away?
She's only got to dream about him – whhtt!! – we're off –
You mark my word – we've got to hold a sacrifice.

SICON: What? *Who's* been dreaming?

GETAS: Oh, you make me tired.

SICON: Come on,
Tell me, who was dreaming?

GETAS: My mistress.

SICON: Well, what was the dream?

GETAS: You'll drive me up the wall. She dreamt that Pan –

SICON: Which Pan?
This one?

75

GETAS: Yes, him.

SICON: Well, what did he do?

GETAS: Why, he got hold
Of Sostratos my master –

SICON: Oh, such a nice young man!

GETAS: – and put chains on his ankles ——

SICON: Apollo! You don't say!

GETAS: Then gave him a leather jacket and a hoe, and told him
To get into that next field and start digging.

SICON: No!!

GETAS: Why, yes! That's what the sacrifice is for, to turn
This 'dreadful portent' into something good.

SICON: I see.
Well, now, pick all those up again and take 'em in;
We'd better rig up the couches, put the place to rights.
Once they get here, I don't want nothing unfortunate
To hold up the sacrifice; everything must go along smooth.
And look here – brighten your face up, can't you, misery?
You'll get your share – I'll stuff you right and proper today.

GETAS: Didn't I always say you was a wonderful man,
And a wonderful cook too? [*Aside*] I don't trust you, all the
same.

[*They both go into the shrine.*]

SECOND CHORAL INTERLUDE

SCENE THREE

CNEMON *comes out, turning to speak to Simice inside.*

CNEMON: Simice, lock the door; and don't you open it
   To anyone till I come back; and I reckon *that*
   Won't be till after dark.
   > [*He is going off to his field when he sees Sostratos' mother
   > and sister arriving with friends and some slaves. He watches
   > them.*]

MOTHER [*to her daughter*]: Come on, you, Plangon, hurry.
   We ought to have got the sacrifice over by now.

CNEMON: Now what on earth's going on here, blast it?
   People again!
   To the crows with them all!

MOTHER: Now, Parthenis, play the Hymn to Pan.
   They say you shouldn't come near Pan without a tune.
   > [*The girl plays.*]

A GUEST: Well, so you've all arrived at last. By Heracles,
   We were getting bored; we've sat about waiting here for
   hours.

MOTHER: Is everything ready for us?

GETAS: Ready? I should say it is.
   That sheep's pretty near died of old age; can't wait for you,
   Poor beast.

MOTHER: Well, come in, everyone; get the baskets ready,
   The holy water, the cakes, the incense!
   > [CNEMON *grunts contemptuously.*]

GETAS [*to Cnemon*]:   Well, old man,
   Have you been struck by lightning? What are you gawp-
   ing at?
   > [*They all crowd into the shrine, leaving* CNEMON
   > *alone.*]

CNEMON: You trash! Damn you to blazes! Can't get on
   with my work.

How can I leave the house, with all that crowd about?
Having this shrine of the Nymphs next door is such a
    plague,
I reckon there's only one thing for it: pull down my house
And build another somewhere else. Look at these thieves
At their sacrifice! They bring in beds, wine by the cask –
For their own pleasure, not the gods'. A bit of incense
Makes a pious gift, or a cake; you offer it in one piece
On the altar, and it all goes to the god. Those gentry there
Offer the gods the inedible scraps – the stump of the tail
And the gall-bladder – and guzzle down all the rest
    themselves.
– You, Simice! Here, open the door again; be quick.
I reckon I'd best keep eye on everything here at home.

       [CNEMON *goes into his house.* GETAS *comes out of the*
       shrine, holding a slave-girl by the arm.]

GETAS: You tell me you've forgotten the kettle, eh? You're
    drunk,
All of you, snoring drunk. *Now* what are we going to do?

       [*The girl runs in.*]

It seems I'll have to bother the god Pan's next-door
    neighbours.

       [*He knocks at Cnemon's door.*]

Hullo, there! – Of all the measly sluts I ever met –
Gods! this lot takes the prize. [*He knocks again.*] Hullo,
    there! – The only thing
They know all about is bed-wrestling. – Anyone in?
– *And* how to blackmail anyone who catches 'em at it.

       [*He continues knocking.*]

Hullo, hullo! – Now what the hell's wrong here? – Hullo!
Isn't there a single slave about? – Ah, that's better;
Someone seems to be coming.

       [CNEMON *opens the door.*]

CNEMON: How dare you touch my door, you cur? How
    dare you, eh?

GETAS: Now, now, don't bite me, there's a good chap.

CNEMON: I will, by God,
    I'll eat you alive.

GETAS: Now, don't, please.

CNEMON: You can't come to *me*
    For money, you damned offal, I don't owe you any.

GETAS: Money nothing – I haven't come to collect a debt;
    Nor have I brought the bailiffs along. I want to borrow
    A kettle.

CNEMON: A kettle?

GETAS: A kettle.

CNEMON: Do you imagine *I*
    Go in for all this nonsense, sacrificing bulls?

GETAS [*aside*]: *You* wouldn't sacrifice a winkle! – *Good*
    afternoon!
    My compliments! The women told me just to knock
    And ask. So I did. It doesn't matter. I'll go back
    And tell them. – Holy gods! Have you ever seen an adder
    With grey hair? Well, here's one.
        [*Exit* GETAS *to the shrine.*]

CNEMON: These brutes, these savages!
    They walk right up and knock at your door like an old
      friend.
    Just let me catch any of you coming to my door again!
    If I don't make him a warning to the whole neighbourhood
    You can call me Simple Simon. That type who came just
      now –
    Whoever he is – how *he* got away with it I don't know.
      [CNEMON *goes back into his house. Enter* SICON *from the*
      shrine followed by GETAS.]

SICON: Damn it, he was telling you what he thought of you.
    Then I'll bet
    You asked him like a stinker. Some people never learn
    To manage a thing like that. Now, *I*'ve mastered the art.
    I go and cook for thousands of people up in town;

I pester their neighbours, borrowing saucepans right and
    left.

If you want anything, you've got to butter 'em up.
    Suppose

An old man answers the door, I say, 'How are you, Dad?'

Or, 'Grandad'; if it's a hag, I call her Ma; or if

She's middle-aged, 'Priestess'; a kitchen-maid I call
    housekeeper.

But you – you're only fit for the rope: you're ignorant.

GETAS: All right. [*He knocks.*] Hullo there, hullo hullo hullo!
    It's me.

Come out here, Dad, I've knocked five times.

CNEMON [*opening the door*]:   What, you again?

GETAS [*dodging behind Sicon*]: Same thing again.

CNEMON: I believe you're plaguing me on purpose.

Didn't I tell you not to come near my door? Here, Simice!

Hand me that strap.

      [GETAS *side-steps, and* CNEMON *beats* SICON.]

SICON: Oh, no! no! Stop!

GETAS [*laughing*]:   Let him go, old boy!

SICON: Let go, for God's sake!

CNEMON: Just you come here again!

SICON: Poseidon

Drown you!

CNEMON: Are you still talking?

SICON [*with an effort, mildly*]:   Listen, I came to ask you

For a large stew-pot.

CNEMON: I haven't got a large stew-pot;

Nor a chopper either; nor salt, vinegar, or anything else.

I've told everyone round here it's absolutely forbidden

To come to my door.

SICON: Not me, you haven't.

CNEMON: I'm telling you now.

SICON [*aside*]: You are, plague rot you. [*To Cnemon*] Please,
    now, listen: wouldn't you just

Inform me where I might get one?

CNEMON: Didn't you hear what I said?
Are you still nattering at me?

SICON: Well, good afternoon.

CNEMON: I can do without 'Good afternoon' from any of
you.

SICON: All right, then, do without it.

CNEMON: Intolerable pests!

[*He goes in, slamming his door.*]

SICON: Whew! Well, he's forked me over properly.

GETAS: See what it is
To ask for things politely. Makes a world of difference.

SICON: Should we knock at another door? If all the people
here
Out clubs as quick as *he* does, I'm going to find things
difficult.
Perhaps I'd best *roast* all the meat. Anyway, I've got
A frying-pan of sorts. Hell to this Phyle crowd!
I'll just use what I've got.

[*Exeunt* SICON *and* GETAS *to the shrine. Enter*
SOSTRATOS *limping and covered with dirt and sweat.*]

SOSTRATOS: If anyone's running short of trouble, just let
him
Come out to Phyle hunting. Oh, my lumbar joints!
They're agony! Oh, my back! My neck! My whole body!
I was a young man, I thought. I threw myself at the work
As soon as I got there, swinging my hoe high in the air
Like any labourer trenching a good crop; I worked –
I gave it all I'd got – for a little while. And then
I began looking around, to see when the old man
Would come with his daughter. And, by Zeus, I took the
chance
To rub the small of my back – without their seeing at first.
As time dragged on and on, I'd bend right over back-
wards –

I was gradually going as stiff as a wooden post.
Nobody came. The sun blazed down. And Gorgias
Watched me out of the corner of his eye, as I gingerly
Straightened up, then over again – up and down
Like a pump-handle. 'Seems to me, young man,' he says,
'Cnemon won't come now.' 'Right,' I said; 'then what do
  we do?'
'Leave it for now,' he said; 'we'll wait for him tomor-
  row.'
Then Daos came to take my place at digging. So –
End of Scene One. Well, here I am – though God knows
  why.
There's something about this business draws me to the
  place.

> [*Enter* GETAS. *He does not at first see Sostratos; he is
> talking to one of the slaves inside the shrine.*]

GETAS: Now what the – here, you! Do you think I've got
  ten pairs of hands?
I make the fire up for you, wash things, carry things,
Cut up the liver, knead the bread, shift everything round,
Keep an eye on the cook. On top of all that I'm blind with
  smoke.
In this feast I reckon I've got the donkey's share.

SOSTRATOS: Getas!
  Hullo there!

GETAS [*rubbing his eyes*]: Who's that?

SOSTRATOS: Me.

GETAS [*pretending not to recognize him*]:   You? Who?

SOSTRATOS: Can't you see me?

GETAS: Why,
  Young master!

SOSTRATOS: Tell me, what are you all doing here?

GETAS: Doing?
  We've just had a sacrifice. Now we're getting a meal
  ready –

For *you*.

SOSTRATOS: Mother here?

GETAS: Long ago.

SOSTRATOS: Father?

GETAS: We're expecting him.

SOSTRATOS: Getas, come over here a moment. In one way
This feast comes in the nick of time. I'm going now
Straight away to find this Gorgias and ask him along,
And his servant too. Once they've shared in our sacrifice,
From then on they're my allies – they'll be much more use
To me in winning Myrrhine.

GETAS: Here, what's this? You'd like
To go and fetch some extra people in to lunch?
Why not? Oh, don't mind *me*. Just make your number up
To a round three thousand. *I'*ll never get so much as a
    bite –
Why should I? I've known that all along. Make it a mass
Meeting. You've sacrificed a splendid animal,
Well worth looking at. But what will our ladies have to
    say?
They're very particular. What do you think *they*'d give
    away
To anyone? Not a pinch of kitchen salt.

SOSTRATOS: Getas,
Don't worry. Today is going to be a great day. I feel it
In my prophetic soul, O Pan! – You see, I always
Say a prayer to you every time I pass your shrine. –
I'll give you a fair deal, Getas.

      [SOSTRATOS *goes to fetch Gorgias and Daos.* SIMICE
      comes out of Cnemon's house.]

SIMICE: Oh, did anyone ever
Have such bad luck? Oh dear, oh dear!

GETAS: Oh, go to hell!

Who's this? Some slut of the old man's.

SIMICE: What'll he do to me?
That bucket that fell down the well – I thought I'd try
To get it out myself, if I could, without saying
Anything to the master. So I got the hoe, to hook
The bucket up with, and let it down on a piece of cord.
Oh dear, the cord was weak and rotten, and it snapped
Straight off.

GETAS: Good work!

SIMICE: So now I've dropped the hoe down there
To join the bucket. Oh dear!

GETAS: All you've got to do now
Is chuck yourself down.

SIMICE: Well, the master, as luck would have it,
Was going to shift a heap of muck out of the yard;
So now he's running in circles, shouting himself hoarse,
Looking for his hoe.

GETAS: That's him coming out. Run for it, now,
You old so-and-so, run! He'll kill you! – Wait; better
stand your ground.

CNEMON [*bursting out*]: Where is she, the old thief?

SIMICE: I didn't mean to, master;
I dropped it down by accident.

CNEMON: Get back indoors.

SIMICE: Now what are you going to do to me?

CNEMON: I'm going to let
You down on a cord.

SIMICE: No, no, no, please!

CNEMON: What's more, by God,
I'm going to use the same cord *you* used for my hoe.
And if it's rotten right through, so much the better.

SIMICE: Help!
I'll call the neighbours, I'll shout for Daos.

CNEMON: Shout for Daos,
Will you, as well as ruin me, you old heathen? Here,

What did I say? Get moving, take your old bones indoors.

      [SIMICE *goes in.*]

CNEMON: What a curse, living alone! – All right, then, *I'*ll go
   down

As soon as the next man. There's no other way.

GETAS: Oh, sir,

   I should be very happy to provide a rope.

CNEMON: You dare provide me anything. I hope the gods
   Make catsmeat of you.

      [CNEMON *goes indoors.*]

GETAS: Serve me right, too, if they did.

   Well, Jack's back in his box. Poor devil, what a life!

   Now, there's pure Attic peasant for you, if you like:

   He fights the stones, for growing nothing but thyme and
      sage,

   And gets no good from it; his only crop is misery.

      [*Enter* SOSTRATOS *with* GORGIAS *and* DAOS.]

   Why, here comes my young master bringing his two
      guests.

   [*With disgust*] Oh! They're just village farm-hands. How
      unsuitable!

   Well! Why does he bring *them* here *now*? And where on
      earth

   Can he have met them?

SOSTRATOS [*to Gorgias*]: Of course you'll come, I insist.
   We've plenty of everything.

   Heracles! What do you call a man who refuses flat

   To come to a feast with his friend after a sacrifice?

   Listen, this is the exact truth: I am your friend,

   And have been since before I first set eyes on you.

   Now, take these hoes and things indoors and then come
      back.

GORGIAS: Oh, but I couldn't. Leave my mother alone at
   home?

SOSTRATOS: Well, do whatever you need to do for her;
   then come.
   I'll meet you here in a minute.
      [*Exit* SOSTRATOS *to the shrine,* GORGIAS *to his
      house.*]

THIRD CHORAL INTERLUDE

SCENE FOUR

SICON *is busy.* SIMICE *runs out of Cnemon's house.*

SIMICE: Help, help! Oh dear, oh dear! Oh gracious me!
  Help, help!
SICON: For Heracles' sake, and all the gods and goddesses!
  Can't you leave us to offer our holy wine in peace?
  All this swearing, beating, screaming – what a house!
SIMICE: My master's down the well!
SICON [*in a dead-pan voice*]: Oh; why?
SIMICE: Why? He was climbing
  Down to fetch out the hoe and the bucket; and he slipped
  Just at the top, and down he went.
SICON [*with delight*]:   Here – you don't mean
  Old Belly-Ache? Not him?
SIMICE: Yes, him.
SICON: You holy gods!
  He never did a better thing. My dear old hag,
  It's up to you now.
SIMICE: What do you mean?
SICON: Just run and find
  A millstone, or a horse-trough – something nice and heavy,
  And tip it down on top of him.
SIMICE: Oh, please, please, my friend,
  Climb down.
SICON: What, *me*? Poseidon! Like the fool in the
    proverb,
  Fight with a mad dog down a well? Not on your life!
SIMICE: Gorgias! Gorgias! Wherever are you?
        [*Enter* GORGIAS *from his house.*]
GORGIAS: Where am I?
  Why, what's the matter, Simice?
SIMICE: Haven't I told you once?

My master's down the well.

    [SOSTRATOS *appears at the entrance of the shrine.*]

GORGIAS: Sostratos, come out here.

SOSTRATOS: Right: into his house, then; lead the way. Go on, hurry.

    [*Exeunt both into Cnemon's house.*]

SICON: Well!! Is there a god in heaven! For Dionysos' sake!

Cnemon, you temple-robber, who won't even lend a kettle

To people who come to sacrifice, you're so damned mean —

Good: now you've fallen down your well, just drink it dry;

Then you won't even have *water* to share with anyone.

The Nymphs have punished him for me, just as he deserved.

No one ever wronged a cook and got away scot-free;

There's something sacred about our art. Now a head-waiter

You can do what you like to, and nothing to fear.

    [MYRRHINE'S *voice is heard indoors.*]

MYRRHINE: Oh dear, oh dear!

He isn't dead, is he? Father darling, are you all right?

SICON: Somebody seems upset. I wonder why. I'm not

The least upset at Cnemon getting soused. What does

Disappoint me is that just when the gods are doing their best

And have brought off something most appropriate, in rush those

Two impious fools to undo it all. I'll bet you, now,

They get a rope and haul the old curmudgeon up.

Eh, gods! What sort of a sight do you think he'll be, all drenched

And shivering? A very pretty sight, you take my word —

And one, friends, that will give me pleasure. Yes, by
    Apollo!
– You ladies, pour libations for them; pray to the gods
For this old man, that he may be spared to end his days
A one-legged cripple. That's the way he'll give least
    trouble
As neighbour to the god Pan and all his worshippers.
It matters to me, in case I'm hired as cook again.

[*Exit* SICON. *Enter* SOSTRATOS.]

SOSTRATOS [*to audience*]: Athenians! By holy Demeter and
    Asclepios,
By all the gods, I never yet in my whole life
Saw any man half-drowned at a more opportune moment.
Oh, we've been having a lovely time! Soon as we got in,
Gorgias jumped straight down the well with a rope, and
    we –
That is, Myrrhine and I – we were above, just doing
Nothing. Well, what was there to do? Except that she
Kept tearing her hair, weeping bitterly, beating her
    breast.
I stood beside her – oh, this is my golden day! –
For all the world as if I'd been her guardian,
Begging, beseeching her to stop, gazing at her –
A vision not of this world. As for the wretched old man
Sputtering away below there, I didn't give him a thought;
Except, of course, that I had to keep hauling on the rope –
And that, I tell you, went dead against the grain. In fact
I very nearly put paid to him: I kept looking
At Myrrhine, and three times or so let the rope slip.
But Gorgias, like the hero that he is, held on,
And in the end I just managed to hoist him up.
Once he was safe, I came out here; I simply couldn't
Control myself any longer – I was on the point
Of going and kissing Myrrhine, I'm so frantically
In love with her. And what I mean to do is this –

There now! I hear them at the door.

[*Enter* GORGIAS *with* CNEMON, *followed by*
MYRRHINE *and* SIMICE.]

                             O Saviour Zeus!

What an apparition!

GORGIAS: Tell me, Cnemon, what can I do
For you?

CNEMON: I don't know. I'm in a terrible state.

GORGIAS: Cheer up.

CNEMON: It's too late to cheer up. You won't have Cnemon
   on your hands
Much longer.

SIMICE: This is what comes of living all alone.

MYRRHINE: You see – you were within an inch of being
   killed
Just now.

GORGIAS: You're an old man. From today on we'll need
To keep an eye on you.

CNEMON: I'm decrepit, yes, I know.
   Gorgias, call your mother here as quick as you can.

      [*Exit* GORGIAS.]

   It seems bad luck's the only thing that can teach us sense.
   Daughter, take hold of me, please; help me on to my feet.

SOSTRATOS: Oh, lucky man!

CNEMON: Why are you standing there? Can't you see I'm
   ill?

SOSTRATOS: I'm waiting . . .

CNEMON: I know, that's what you said before. Clear
   off!

     [SOSTRATOS *retires to corner of stage.* GORGIAS *returns*
     with CNEMON'S WIFE.]

GORGIAS: Here she is, Cnemon, my mother.

WIFE: Oh, dear, is he badly hurt?

CNEMON: Is that my wife?

WIFE: Yes, here I am.

CNEMON: Don't chatter, then. I want to say
  Several things to all of you together, while they're on my
    mind.
  Listen, wife, and Myrrhine and Gorgias. I tell you this:
  I'd much rather have been killed outright –
    [*They make deprecating noises.*]
                            Yes! Nor could any of you
  Ever make me change my mind about it; so agree with me.
  One mistake, perhaps, I *have* made – thought I could do
    everything
  For myself, be independent, ask no help from anyone.
  Now I've seen that life may have a swift and unexpected
    end –
  Well, I know I was mistaken. Every man needs someone
    near,
  Needs a friend he knows will help him. But, when I saw
    people's lives
  All absorbed in making money, watched them scheme and
    calculate,
  By Hephaestos, I grew bitter. Not a single man, I thought,
  Ever has true kindly feeling towards another. This idea
  Paralysed me. Only now has one man proved the con-
    trary –
  Gorgias, whose action shows a generous and noble heart.
  There I was – I even forbade him ever to come near my
    door;
  Never raised a hand to help him; never even talked to him,
  Never said Good morning. Yet, from mere good will, he
    saved my life.
  Others would have said – and justly, 'Since you've told me
    to keep out,
  Right, I'll keep out; since you've never helped me – right,
    I won't help *you*.'
  Now look here, my boy; whether I die now, as I think I
    shall –

I'm in a bad way – or whether I get over it, I adopt you
now
As my son. My money, and my whole estate, consider
yours.
As for my daughter Myrrhine, I entrust her to you. You
must find
A husband for her. I should never manage to find her one
myself,
Even if I had my health – there isn't one that I should ever
like.
You just let me live my own life. Take the whole place
over, son.
You've got sense; and good luck to you. You're the
natural guardian
For your sister. Reckon up the value of my property;
Give her one half for her dowry; take the other half your-
self,
And look after me and your mother.

                        Lay me down now, Myrrhine.
Talking more than necessary is no occupation for a man;
But there's just one thing I'd like to say to you, son, in
defence
Of myself, my way of living. In a word, if everyone
Followed *my* way, did as I do, soon there'd be no courts of
law,
Nor would men put men in prisons, nor fight wars; but
each would have
What he needed, and be satisfied. Ah, well; people like it
best,
I suppose, the way things are now; carry on, then, as you
were.
One cantankerous old man will soon be well out of your
way.

GORGIAS: Father, thank you for all you've said. Now the
first thing we have to do,

With your help, is find a man for Myrrhine – if you agree.

CNEMON: I've told you what *I* want. Don't fuss *me* about it,
for God's sake.

GORGIAS: Here's a young man wants to meet you –

CNEMON: For the gods' sake, *no*!

GORGIAS: – to ask
You for leave to marry Myrrhine.

CNEMON: Who? – I'm finished with all that;
Can't be bothered.

GORGIAS: It's the man who helped to save your life.

CNEMON: Who's that?

GORGIAS: Here he is. Come, Sostratos.

[SOSTRATOS *comes forward.*]

CNEMON: He's sunburnt. Is he a farmer, then?

GORGIAS: I should think so! He's not soft; he's not the sort of
man you'll find
Ambling round all day doing nothing.

CNEMON: Very well. You'll find indoors
One gold talent: that's her dowry. Give her to this man.
Arrange
For a decent, proper wedding. Carry me indoors.

GORGIAS: I will do
Everything you say. Here, Simice, take him in; look after
him.

[SIMICE *helps* CNEMON *back into the house.*]

SOSTRATOS: Gorgias: to complete the pattern, take *my* sister
for *your* wife.

GORGIAS: Let's consider that another time, my friend.

SOSTRATOS: Why, Gorgias,
There's no obstacle; my father won't oppose me in anything.

GORGIAS: Well . . . At least I here betroth and give you,
before these witnesses,
Myrrhine; so take and keep her, brother, as your lawful
wife.

When you came to court her, you used no pretence. You
    were prepared
Honestly to do anything to win her. Though your hands
    were soft,
You took a hoe, and dug – went through it willingly. A
    thing like that
Shows what stuff a man is made of, when he can forget his
    wealth,
Take his coat off, and work side by side with a poor
    countryman.
Such a man will bear the ups and downs of life with a good
    heart.
You've shown clearly enough what sort of chap you are.
    Well, stay like this
All your life.

SOSTRATOS: I hope to be a *better* man than I am now.
    Still, self-praise is in poor taste. – Why, look! How very
    fortunate!
    Here's my father.

GORGIAS [*recognizing him*]: Callippides! Is *he* your father?

SOSTRATOS: Certainly.

GORGIAS: Is he, now? He's a rich man, by Zeus; and he de-
    serves to be.
He's a first-rate farmer.

      [*Enter* CALLIPPIDES; *he does not at first see the others.*]

CALLIPPIDES: I've arrived too late, no doubt. They've all
    Long ago devoured the sheep, and vanished round the
    countryside.

GORGIAS [*aside to Sostratos*]: Why, he's starving, by Poseidon!
    Is this quite the moment to –
    Talk to him?

SOSTRATOS [*aside to Gorgias*]: No; let him eat first – he'll be
    more amenable.

      [GORGIAS' MOTHER *and* MYRRHINE *retire into*
      Cnemon's house.]

CALLIPPIDES: Sostratos! Well, what's going on here? Have
you eaten?

SOSTRATOS: Yes, father;
But there's plenty left for you, so come on in.

CALLIPPIDES [*going towards the shrine*]:   I will indeed.

GORGIAS [*aside to Sostratos*]: Go in with him. Say what you
have to say between the two of you.

SOSTRATOS: Will you wait for me indoors, then?

GORGIAS: Yes, yes, I'll not leave the house.

SOSTRATOS: Right you are, then. Won't take long. I'll come
and call you very soon.

　　　[*Exeunt* SOSTRATOS *and* GORGIAS.]

FOURTH CHORAL INTERLUDE

SCENE FIVE

CALLIPPIDES *and* SOSTRATOS *come out of the shrine.*

SOSTRATOS: Father, your attitude leaves me not quite
    satisfied;
  In fact, a little disappointed.
CALLIPPIDES: Why? Haven't I
  Agreed that you shall marry the girl you love? I mean it;
  And I insist upon it.
SOSTRATOS: *I* don't think you mean it.
CALLIPPIDES: Now by the gods I do. You're young; I see
    this marriage
  As helping you to settle down – if it is love
  That leads you to your choice.
SOSTRATOS: Well, since I'm going to marry
  Gorgias' sister, because I think him worthy of
  Our family, why do you now say you won't give *him*
  My sister in return?
CALLIPPIDES: It's a frightful suggestion!
  What? Get a daughter-in-law and a son-in-law together
  Both penniless? I've no wish to. One is quite enough.
SOSTRATOS: You talk of money: money's unpredictable.
  If you are certain money's going to stay by you
  All through your life, then guard it close, let no one else
  Touch any of it, keep control in your own hands.
  But if it all belongs to Fortune, not to you,
  Father, why should you grudge a share to anyone?
  Fortune herself may well rob you of all you have
  And give it to someone else who perhaps doesn't deserve
    it.
  So I say, as long as you possess your money, father,
  You ought to use it generously yourself, and put it
  At everyone's disposal, and make as many people

Rich as you possibly can. That's something permanent;
And when *you*'re in trouble, that's where you'll find help
in turn.
A friend for everyone to see is worth far more
Than money shut out of sight or buried down the garden.

CALLIPPIDES: Look here, my son, you know me. The
money I've put together
I don't keep buried away for myself. Well, what do you
think?
It all belongs to you. So, if you want to invest
In a friend for the future, use your judgement, go ahead,
And I wish you all good luck. Why moralize to me?
Go and be generous; give away, or share; I've changed
My mind, I'm with you, willingly.

SOSTRATOS: Yes? Willingly?

CALLIPPIDES: Indeed, yes; have no qualms.

SOSTRATOS: Then I'll call Gorgias.

GORGIAS [*appearing*]: I was just at the door, on the point of
coming out,
And I heard every word you said, right from the start.
Now, Sostratos, I know you're a warm-hearted friend;
And I'm extremely fond of you. But I don't want
A style of life above my own; even if I did
Want it – by Zeus, I couldn't stand it.

SOSTRATOS: I don't see
Quite what you mean.

GORGIAS: Don't you? I'm giving you my
sister
To be your wife. But as for *my* marrying *your* sister –
It's kind of you, but –

SOSTRATOS: Why not?

GORGIAS: Well, I don't much care
To live like a rich man on what someone else has earned.
I'd rather earn it for myself.

SOSTRATOS: Why, Gorgias,

97

You're talking nonsense. Do you think you're not good
  enough
To marry my sister?

GORGIAS: Yes, I think I'm good enough;
  But it's not right for a man who only has a little
  To take a lot.

CALLIPPIDES: By Zeus almighty, I like the tone
  Of the rubbish you talk.

GORGIAS: How?

CALLIPPIDES: You're a have-not, and you mean
  To appear a have-not. However, since, as you see, my
  son
  Has managed to persuade me – come, use common sense.

GORGIAS: Your arguments convince me from two sides at
  once.
  If a man has neither money to show nor common sense
  Folk soon think there's no hope for him. – All right, I
  agree.
  It only remains to make our contract formally.

  [CALLIPPIDES' WIFE and DAUGHTER enter from
  the shrine.]

CALLIPPIDES: Young man, I now solemnly promise and
  betroth
  My daughter to you, to bear you lawful sons; and give
  With her a dowry of three talents.

GORGIAS: And I have
  One talent to give as dowry with Myrrhine.

CALLIPPIDES: You have?
  Now, don't offer too much.

GORGIAS: I have it.

CALLIPPIDES: Well, I accept
  The talent as her dowry. Don't divide the farm;
  Keep it yourself, Gorgias, intact. Now fetch your mother
  And sister here to meet our womenfolk.

GORGIAS: Yes, of course.

SOSTRATOS: Good. Now, tonight we'll all stay here and have
    a feast.
  Tomorrow we'll have the weddings. – Oh, and Gorgias,
    bring
  Old Cnemon here too. He needs looking after; perhaps
  We can do more for him.
GORGIAS: No, he won't come, Sostratos.
SOSTRATOS: Oh, but persuade him.
GORGIAS: If I can.
        [*Exit* GORGIAS.]
SOSTRATOS: Now, father dear,
  We must arrange a splendid drinking-party for *us*,
  And keep the ladies awake all night.
CALLIPPIDES: On the contrary,
  The ladies'll do the drinking, of that I'm very sure,
  And *we*'ll be kept awake all night. Oh, well; I'll go
  And get ready what's necessary for you.
SOSTRATOS: Do.
  [*To audience*] There isn't any single thing an honest
    worker
  Ought ever to despair of. Diligence and hard work
  Will get you everything. Look at *me*, now: in one day
  I have achieved a marriage beyond all men's dreams.
        [GORGIAS *approaches with his* MOTHER *and*
        MYRRHINE.]
GORGIAS: Come on, now, quickly, both of you.
SOSTRATOS: Yes, please come. Mother,
  Will you receive these ladies? Where's Cnemon?
GORGIAS: Sostratos,
  Cnemon still won't come. He was even begging us
  To send old Simice away, so that he could be
  Entirely alone and by himself.
SOSTRATOS: Well, what a man!
GORGIAS: He's like that.
SOSTRATOS: Then forget him. Come on, let's be going.

GORGIAS: I'm much too shy to meet these ladies, Sostratos.

SOSTRATOS: Oh, nonsense! Come on. Mother, this is
　　Gorgias.
　　[*To Gorgias*] Remember, from today we're all one family.
　　　　　　[*They all go into the shrine.* SIMICE *comes out of
　　　　　　Cnemon's house, shouting back at him.*]

SIMICE: I *am*, by Artemis, I'm going too. Just you
　　Lie there and stew in your own bad temper, all alone.
　　These gentlefolk all want to take you to the shrine,
　　And you say No. By the two goddesses, you'll have
　　Another dreadful accident, much worse than this.
　　. . . Well, I hope you'll be all right.
　　　　　　[GETAS *comes from the shrine.*]
　　　　　　　　　　　　Why, Getas, where are you going?

GETAS: I'm going in to the old man, to see if he needs any-
　　thing.
　　　　　　[*The sound of flute-music comes from the shrine.*]
　　Now, damn you, what's the use of playing the flute to *me*,
　　I ask you?
　　I've no time yet to go and dance. They've sent me here to
　　visit
　　The patient, see? Keep quiet.

SIMICE: 　　　　That's right, *you* sit with him. It's high time
　　For someone else to take a turn. I'm going to my young
　　mistress
　　To say good-bye, and kiss her and talk to her, and give my
　　blessing.

GETAS: Of course you must; trot off. Meanwhile *I'll* give him
　　proper treatment.
　　　　　　[*Exit* SIMICE.]
　　I've long been wanting such a chance, but couldn't see how
　　to work it.
　　No one can come out yet awhile, they're all too busy
　　drinking.
　　　　　　[*He goes to the door of the shrine and calls softly.*]

Hey, cook! Hey, Sicon! Come out here, come quickly!
 [SICON *appears*.]

            O Poseidon!

Guess what a treat I've got for you.

SICON [*rather drunk*]:   You called me?

GETAS: Yes, I called you.

 The things *he* did to you just now – do you want to get your
  own back?

SICON: Did things to me just now? What things? You're
 talking through your arse, boy.

GETAS: Old Belly-Ache's asleep, alone.

SICON: And what is his [*hiccup*] condition?

GETAS: Not half so sick as he might be.

SICON: Could he get on his feet and beat us?

GETAS: Couldn't even get on his feet, I reckon.

SICON: Sounds delightful!

 I'll go right in and ask for something; that'll send him
  raving!

GETAS: Wait; first let's lug the man out here; then, when
 we've got him planted,

 Let's bang like blazes on his door, and ask for things, and
  drive him

 Into a flaming temper. That will be some pleasure, I tell you.

SICON: It's Gorgias I'm afraid of; if he catches us he'll flay us.

GETAS: Hark at the row in there – they're drinking; no one's
 going to hear us.

 In fact, it's up to us, now that the old boy's a relation,

 To teach him family manners. If his present style continues

 It's no joke to put up with.

SICON: It is not.

GETAS [*opening the door*]:   Be very careful

 To get him out in front here without anybody seeing.

  [*He pushes Sicon in front of him.*]

 Go on a bit, now.

SICON: Wait, I implore you – now don't go and leave me;

And for the gods' sake don't make noises.

GETAS: I never made no noises.
Swear by the earth I didn't.

> [*They carry Cnemon out asleep in his chair.*]
>
>   To your right.

SICON: There we are.

GETAS: Put him down now.
Now's the moment.

SICON: I'll go first. Look – you repeat my rhythm.

> [*He knocks as follows: tum-túm-ti-tum, tum-túm-ti-tum, tum-túm.*]

CNEMON [*muttering in his sleep*]:   Oh, help, I'm done for!

GETAS: Now me.

> [*He knocks, in the same rhythm.*]

CNEMON [*waking*]: Oh, help! I'm done for! [*He sees Sicon.*]
Who's that? You're one of that crowd, I can see you are.
Now what are you after?

> [SICON *is shouting into the house, not looking at* CNEMON, *who is outside.*]

SICON: Please, sir, I want to borrow a kettle *and* a pudding-basin.

CNEMON [*growling ominously*]: Oh, someone help me up.

SICON: You've got one, I know for sure you've got one.
And I want seven saucepans, *and* twelve tables. Slaves, look sharp now
And take my message, I'm in a hurry.

CNEMON: I've got nothing.

SICON: Nothing?

CNEMON: Nothing, I've told you a thousand times.

SICON: I'm off, then.

CNEMON: Plagues and devils!
How did I get out here? Who stuck me down out here?
Clear off, you!

GETAS [*knocking twice as loudly*]: Now my turn. Porter!
Butlers!

Housemaids! PORTER!!

CNEMON: You – you madman!
You'll smash my door in.

GETAS: Lend me nine hearth-rugs.

CNEMON: Where from?

GETAS: I want too
Some woven Persian hangings – thirty yards.

CNEMON: I wish I had 'em.

GETAS: You've got them.

CNEMON: Where? Simice! Oh, where's that old crone?

GETAS: I'm going
To try at another door.

CNEMON: Clear off, then. Simice!

        [SICON *comes up again.*]

                            You devil,
May all the gods torment you! What do you want?

SICON: I want to borrow
A large bronze stewing-pan.

CNEMON [*nearly bursting*]:   Oh, someone help me up!

GETAS [*coming back*]:   I'm certain
You've got those Persian hangings, Dad, quite certain of it.

CNEMON: I haven't.

SICON: No? nor the stew-pan neither?

CNEMON: I'll kill that Simice.

        [SIMICE *suddenly reappears from the shrine.* GETAS *and*
        SICON *run to hide at the edge of the stage.*]

SIMICE [*derisively*]:   Go to sleep, now;
Stop growling. Look at you – a man who avoids his fellow
    creatures,
Hates his own wife –

        [GETAS *and* SICON, *seeing Simice is on their side,*
        return.]

                        – and won't join in at a sacrifice or a party.
So take your medicine, all of it.

SICON: There's no one here to help you.

GETAS: Sit there and stew in your own juice.

SIMICE: And listen to your misdoings
All set out in order.

CNEMON: I won't listen. I've done nothing.
I only ask to be left alone to live the way I want to.
I interfere with nobody. Although I'm ill and helpless
I didn't even make my daughter stay at home to attend
me.
In any case, what good have she and her mother got from
going?

SIMICE: They're being congratulated and embraced by all the
neighbours –
A most delightful experience for your poor wife and
daughter.

SICON: Why, over there I was laying out a feast for all those
people –

GETAS: You listening, hey? Now don't drop off.

CNEMON: Drop off! Great gods!

GETAS: What about it?
Will you come to the party?

SICON: Listen, I'll tell you some more.
We were in a hurry;
And I was strewing the ground with mats and cushions,
setting the tables –
Yes, me. Are you listening? That's my business, I'm a cook
by profession.

GETAS: Don't you remember?

SICON: The man's no spirit.

GETAS: Someone else was lifting
And tipping into the mixing-bowl a jar of Jolly Bacchos
Of ancient vintage; stirring in water from the Nymphs'
fountain,
And drinking healths with the men –

SICON: – while someone else filled up for the women;
Like pouring wine into sand, it was.

SIMICE: Ah! Can you picture it, Cnemon?
A little slave-girl, rather merry, wearing a wreath of ivy
To crown the flower of her young face; her feet already
    restless
With the rhythm; shyly hesitating, fluttering with excite-
    ment:
Another girl joins hands with her, and away they dance
    together!

GETAS: Cnemon, you've had a terrible time – now come on,
    join the dancers!
    [*He takes Cnemon by the arm to lift him up.*]

CNEMON: What are you up to? Hit me, would you?

GETAS: No! Just come and join them.

SICON: You've got no manners!

CNEMON: I won't, I swear.

GETAS: All right – do we have to carry you?

CNEMON: Oh, what can I do?

SICON: Dance, man!

CNEMON: I suppose perhaps it'll be less painful
To dance in there than endure you here.

GETAS: You're right! We've won! It's a triumph!
Here, Donax, Sicon, Syros, all you slaves, come here!
    [*A number of slaves run up.*]
Right: pick him up and carry him in.
    [*They pick Cnemon up in his chair.*]
                                    Cnemon: look out
For yourself, if ever we catch you making trouble for
    us;
I swear we'll give you the *full* treatment another time.
    [*Some guests come out to welcome them in.*]
Give us garlands, someone, and a torch.
    [*A garland is put on Cnemon's head, a torch in his hand.
    Guests form a procession round him.*]
                                    Now, up with him!
    [*They lift him high and carry him in to the dancing.*]

So, now we've brought to heel this troublesome old man,
Congratulate us, all of you, both young and old,
And give us a hearty clap. May noble Victory,
The laughter-loving maiden, stay our friend for ever!

EPITREPONTES
OR
THE ARBITRATION

CHARACTERS

ONESIMOS, *a slave of Charisios*
DAOS, *a shepherd*
SMICRINES, *father of Pamphile, wife of Charisios*
SYRISCOS, *a charcoal-burner, slave of Chaerestratos*
HABROTONON, *a guitar-girl*
CHAERESTRATOS, *a rich Athenian, father of Charisios*
PAMPHILE, *wife of Charisios*
SOPHRONE, *Pamphile's nurse, an old slave of Smicrines*
CHARISIOS, *a young man*
CHORUS *of Banqueters*
Syriscos' wife; an infant in arms

★

The place is near Athens; and the scene shows two houses. One is that of Charisios, where Pamphile is now living; the other belongs to Chaerestratos, and here his son Charisios is living with Habrotonon.

Act 1[1]

SCENE ONE

ONESIMOS *and* DAOS *meet*.

DAOS: I say, Onesimos, do tell me: is it true
    That your young master Charisios, who is living here
    With this guitar-girl Habrotonon, is in fact
    A quite recently married man?
ONESIMOS: I'm sorry to say
    That's perfectly true.

---

1. Of this Act only three lines are preserved.

Act 2

SCENE ONE

SYRISCOS *enters from the country with his wife, who is carrying a baby; they are met by* DAOS, *who is coming from Athens. Syriscos has just demanded of Daos the ornaments which, he has been told, were found with the child; and Daos has refused to give them up.*

SYRISCOS: You're evading your duty.

DAOS: And you're trying to swindle me,
   You perisher.

SYRISCOS: You've no right to keep what isn't yours.

DAOS: Look – arbitration! That's the thing! We must get someone
   To arbitrate for us.

SYRISCOS: I'm ready.

DAOS: Good; let's get this settled.

SYRISCOS: Who shall we ask?

DAOS: Anyone you like will do for me.
   – Shall I get my rights, though? Oh, why on earth did I ever
   Tell you about it?

       [SMICRINES, *who has been visiting his daughter Pamphile in Charisios' house, now comes out.*]

SYRISCOS: Would you agree to have *him* as judge?

DAOS: That's lucky. Yes, have him.

SYRISCOS [*to Smicrines*]:   My good sir, excuse me, sir!
   Could you, if you please, spare us a few moments, sir?

SMICRINES: Spáre you a few moments? What's it about?

SYRISCOS: You see, we're having
   A bit of an argument.

SMICRINES: What has that got to do with me?

SYRISCOS: Why, this: we're both looking for some fair-minded person
   To decide it for us. If nothing urgent calls you away
   This moment, you arbitrate for us!

SMICRINES: You slippery rogues!
So you parade the streets making lawyers' speeches, do you?
Hob-nail boots and all, eh?

SYRISCOS: Well, what if we do?
It's quite a simple argument, Dad, won't take you a minute.
Come on; we'd be greatly obliged to you. And please don't say
A thing like this doesn't matter. Justice ought to prevail
Everywhere and on all occasions. The passer-by
Ought to feel it's his duty to see justice done.
It's one of life's obligations – comes to everybody.

DAOS [aside]: Eh, now I've got tangled up with a right speechifier.
Why did I ever say a single word to him?

SMICRINES: Now tell me, are you both going to abide by my decision?

SYRISCOS: Certainly we are.

SMICRINES: I'll hear you then; why shouldn't I?
[To Daos] Well, you've said nothing so far. Come on, you speak first.

DAOS: I'll have to begin a little way back, before my quarrel
With him began, so that you can get the whole thing clear.
Well, sir: about a month ago I was with my sheep
On the heath not far from here; on that particular day
I was all alone. And there, lying on the scrub, I found
A little new-born child, with tokens round its neck,
Ornaments, and such things.

SYRISCOS: Those are what the quarrel's about.

DAOS: See? He won't let me speak!

SMICRINES: If you interrupt again
You'll feel my stick, see?

DAOS: Quite right, too.

SMICRINES: Speak on.

DAOS: I will.
I picked the child up; took it home, with all its things.

I'd a mind to rear it – seemed a good idea just then.
But in the night I had second thoughts, as people do.
'Children mean trouble; what about the expense?' I thought,
'And all the worry?' That's the way I looked at it.
Next morning, out with the sheep again. *He* comes along
To the same place – he's a charcoal-burner – to saw logs.
I'd known him a long time. We started talking. He
Saw I was gloomy. 'What's the matter, Daos?' he says.
'You've something on your mind.' 'I'm a busybody,' I
   said;
And I told him all about it; how I'd found the child
And taken it home. Then straight away, before I'd finished
'Please now,' he said, 'if ever you hope for blessing, Daos,' –
Those were his very words – 'if you hope for luck, for
   freedom,
Give *me* the child. I've got a wife,' he said; 'she had
A baby, who died.' That's his wife there, holding the child.

SMICRINES [*to Syriscos*]: Did you say this?

SYRISCOS: I did, yes.

DAOS: Why, he gave me no peace
The whole day long, begging and arguing. At last
I agreed; gave him the child; and off he went, praying
For blessings on me – kissed my hands as he took the kid.

SMICRINES [*to Syriscos*]: Is that true?

SYRISCOS: Quite true.

DAOS: That was that. But now today
He happens to meet me here, with his wife, and suddenly
He wants the things I found laid out beside the child –
Just worthless bits and pieces – demands them as his right;
Very indignant that I refuse to give them up.
By right, I say, they're mine. He asked for the child, and
   got it;
He ought to be grateful. Why should I be put on trial
For not giving him everything? If he'd been there
With me, and shared the luck of the find, then naturally

Part would have gone to him, and part to me; but I
Found it alone. Now, do you think you should have the lot,
And me nothing at all, when you weren't even there?
It comes to this: I made you a free gift of what
Was mine. If you're contented, keep it. If you're not,
If you've now changed your mind, give the child back to
    me.
That means no injury or loss to you. But if
You claim the lot, part as a willing gift, and part
By forcing me, you're in the wrong. Well, that's my case.
SYRISCOS: Has he finished?
SMICRINES: Didn't you hear? He's finished.
SYRISCOS: Good, my turn.
His story's quite true – he alone found the child; no doubt
Of that, that's how it happened, sir, I don't dispute.
I asked and begged him for it; and he gave it me –
All true. Now, he told one of his mates, another shepherd,
That he'd found certain tokens with the child. This man
Told me. Now, sir, this infant – Give him to me, wife –

[*Syriscos takes the child from his wife.*]

Comes here himself to claim them. Daos, he demands
His necklace, and the other tokens of his birth.
They were put on him, he says, to bring him credit, not
To keep you fed. By giving him to me, you yourself
Made me his guardian. As his guardian, then, I join
With him in asking for his rights.

[*He gives the child back to his wife.*]

                        So now, sir, this,
I reckon, is what you must decide: whether this gold,
Or whatever the tokens are, ought to be kept for him
Until he grows up (since his mother, whoever she was,
Gave them with that intention) or whether this man here,
Who robbed him of them, ought to keep what isn't his
Because he found him first. – You, Daos, may wonder why
I didn't ask for these tokens at the time, when you

Gave me the child. Why, at that time I had no right
To speak for him. Even now I ask nothing for myself.
You say you 'shared the luck of the find' with me. You
    call it
A 'find'? You stripped this body! That's no 'find'; that's
    theft.
    A further point, sir: this young boy here is, perhaps,
Of noble birth, and will in time look far beyond
Us working folk that reared him; rise to his own level,
Perform some exploit worthy of his blood; hunt lions,
Bear arms in battle, run in the Olympic games.
You've seen plays in the theatre – you know all those tales
By heart – Neleus and Pelias, how they were found
By an old goat-herd wearing the kind of leather coat
I'm wearing now; when he saw the boys were of better
    stock
Than himself, he told them the whole story, how he'd found
And taken them home; and he gave them the little leather
    bag
Of tokens, from which they learnt the truth about their
    birth;
And so, brought up as goat-herds, they became both kings.
Now, suppose Daos had grabbed those tokens and sold the
    lot
To put twelve drachmas in his pocket: the two princes,
Both noble heroes, would have lived their whole lives
    unknown.
    Now, sir: is it right that *I* should house, clothe, feed this
    child,
While Daos takes and throws away his only hope
Of a good life? Tokens like these have held men back
From incest, helped them recognize and save from death
Parent or brother. Danger's a part of human life;
Then, sir, we should take care, and value every means
To overcome it. 'Give the child back,' Daos says,

'If you're not satisfied.' Now there he thinks he has
A powerful argument. It's not a just one, though.
Because you owe this child his property, do you now want
To take the child himself? Perhaps you think you'd feel
Safer for the next piece of dirty work – selling
The bits and pieces Fortune has preserved for him?
   I've finished. Give whatever decision you think right.

SMICRINES: The case is clear. All articles exposed with the
   child
Are the child's property. That's my judgement.

DAOS: Good; but who
Is to have the child?

SMICRINES: Certainly not the man who now
Wrongs him, but his defender and champion against you
Who tried to rob him.

SYRISCOS: Bless you, bless you, sir!

DAOS: What? Zeus!
That's a disgraceful judgement! I found everything,
I alone; and now I'm stripped of everything; this man
Found nothing, takes the lot! Must I hand over, then?

SMICRINES: You must.

DAOS: It's scandalous, damned if it isn't.

SYRISCOS: Come on, quick now.

DAOS: Outrageous! Heracles!

SYRISCOS: Untie that wallet, show us the things –
That's where you carry them. [*To Smicrines, who is going*]
   Sir, I beg you, wait here a minute
To make sure he hands over.

DAOS: Oh! Why did I ever agree
To let him judge?

SYRISCOS: Come on, now, handcuffs, part with it.

DAOS [*giving the wallet*]: It's shameful.

SMICRINES: Is it all there?

SYRISCOS: I think so.

SMICRINES: So do I –

Unless he swallowed this or that while I was giving
Judgement against him.

SYRISCOS: I hardly think he could do that.
  Well, best of luck, sir! If only all judgements were as just!
      [*Exit* SMICRINES.]

DAOS: Heracles! Of all the stupid, scandalous decisions!

SYRISCOS: You're a bad lot.

DAOS: You thief! I'll keep an eye on you
  Day and night from now on, to see you guard those things
  And keep them safe for the child.

SYRISCOS: Shog off and drown yourself.
      [*Exit* DAOS *towards the country.*]

Wife, hold this wallet; take it into my master's house.[1]
Right. Now we'll wait here for Chaerestratos. Tomorrow,
When I've paid my monthly dues, we'll set off back to work.
But first let's make a note of these things one by one.
Got a basket? Well, hold out your gown.

> [SYRISCOS *tips the contents of the wallet into his wife's
> gown.* ONESIMOS *enters from Chaerestratos' house; he
> looks up and down the road.* SYRISCOS, *who is busy
> looking through the articles from the wallet, does not see
> him at first.*]

ONESIMOS: Cooks always arrive late. This one's the worst
  I've known.
Yesterday by this time the meal was finished with.

SYRISCOS: This seems to be a sort of chicken. A tough one
  too.
Take it. What's this now? Something set with stones. And
  here's
A toy axe.

ONESIMOS [*to himself*]: What's going on?

SYRISCOS: Look, here's a signet-ring;
  Gold-plate on iron; and the device, a bull or goat –

---

1. Does he want them given to Chaerestratos, or Charisios, for safe-keeping?

I can't tell which ... Some letters – here's the maker's name,
  Cleostratos.

ONESIMOS [*excited*]: Here! Show me.

SYRISCOS: There. Who are you?

ONESIMOS: It is!

  The very one.

SYRISCOS: What is?

ONESIMOS: This ring.

SYRISCOS: Is what? I don't

  Know what you're talking about.

ONESIMOS: This is Charisios' ring,

  My master's.

SYRISCOS: Oh, you're crazy.

ONESIMOS [*slipping it on his finger*]: The one he lost.

SYRISCOS: Look here,

  Give that ring back, you miserable –

ONESIMOS: Give it back, eh? It's ours!

  And where did you get it from?

SYRISCOS: You twister! Holy gods,

  It's a lovely job, looking after an orphan's property!
  First man you meet'll rob you as soon as look at you.
  Give me that ring, I tell you. Are you being funny with
    me?

ONESIMOS: This is my master's ring, I swear it by all the gods.

SYRISCOS: I'll be hanged, drawn and quartered before I
    haggle with you.

  All right, then, let 'em all come. I'll take every man of them
  To a court of law. It's not my property, it's the boy's.
  Wife, take this necklace; this red wrapper. Now, indoors!

      [*His wife goes into Chaerestratos' house, taking the child
      and the rest of the tokens.*]

  Now, you: what have you got to say?

ONESIMOS: This ring belongs

  To Charisios my master. He lost it when he was drunk,
  So he told me.

SYRISCOS: I see. Well, I belong to Chaerestratos.
    Either keep that safe, or give it to him; whichever you like.
ONESIMOS: I've got it safe; I'd rather take charge of it myself.
SYRISCOS: It doesn't matter to me. In any case we both
    Seem to be going to the same house.
ONESIMOS: But at this moment
    Guests are arriving – not a good time, perhaps, to mention
    This to my master. Tomorrow.
SYRISCOS: I can wait. Tomorrow
    I'm ready to put my case before any judge you like.
            [*Exit* ONESIMOS *into Chaerestratos' house.*]
    Well! Didn't come off too badly with him either. These days
    You've got to set everything else aside, and go to law.
    Seems it's the only way a man can assert his rights.
            [*Exit* SYRISCOS *to the house in pursuit of Onesimos.
            Some of Charisios' guests arrive and present the* SECOND
            CHORAL INTERLUDE; *after which they too retire into
            the same house.*]

Act 3

SCENE ONE

Enter ONESIMOS *from Chaerestratos' house, furtively; he is keeping out of Syriscos' way.*

ONESIMOS [*to the audience*]: See this ring here: five times or
    more I've started off
To show it to Charisios my master; I go to him,
And then, as soon as I'm standing right in front of him,
I shirk it. I wish now I'd never told him anything
About his wife having a child while he was away.[1]
Ten times a day I hear him muttering, 'Blast the man
Who told me that!' I'm terrified that he and his wife
Will make it up; and since I'm the man who knows what
    happened,
And tipped him off, he'll just make a clean sweep of me.
Well, then, I'd best brew up some other kettle of fish; –
Yet that, again, involves a terrible risk for me.

      [HABROTONON *appears at Chaerestratos' door, pro-*
      testing to some young men inside who are molesting her –
      no doubt guests of Charisios.]

HABROTONON: Let go, now, please! Stop! Will you please
    leave me alone?

      [*The young men vanish.* HABROTONON *speaks to the*
      audience, standing on the opposite side of the stage to
      ONESIMOS, *who is still looking at the ring and does not*
      notice her.]

Well, of all the wretched luck! I've made a fool of myself.
How was I to know? I expected to be made love to;
But the man hates me – it's unnatural, the way he hates me!
Why, now he won't even have me next to him at dinner;

---

1. This line is not in the Greek; since much of the play is missing it is necessary to add some explanation here.

119

I'm put at a distance.

ONESIMOS: Am I to give it back again
To the fellow I've just taken it from? Ridiculous!

HABROTONON: But why does he pour out money for nothing
  so recklessly?
For all he's done, poor chap, I could this very moment
Carry a holy basket in the Panathenaea;
I've been here three days now, and I'm still, as the priest
  says,
A pure and untouched virgin.

ONESIMOS: And if I don't, then how on earth, for the gods'
  sake – ?

      [*Enter* SYRISCOS *from a side door of Chaerestratos'
      house.* HABROTONON *listens unseen.*]

SYRISCOS: I'm chasing him round in circles. Where's he got
  to? [*Seeing Onesimos*] Hey!
You in the porch there!

      [ONESIMOS *turns and comes up to him.*]

                  Listen, friend: either give that ring
Back to me now, or show it without more waste of time
To the man you want to show it to. I've got things to do;
Let's settle the matter.

ONESIMOS: Look, mate, this is the position.
This ring's my master Charisios' ring, I know it is;
But I don't want to show it him. If I hand him this,
Found with the foundling child, why, I as good as make
Him the child's father.

SYRISCOS: How do you mean, you fool?

ONESIMOS: Listen.
He lost this ring last year at the Tauropolia –
An all-night song-and-dance for women. It's pretty clear
What happened was, a girl got raped, and had this child;
And then, of course, exposed it. Now, if someone could
First find the girl, and then produce this ring, he'd have

Clear proof; but now, showing the ring would only cause
Suspicion and confusion.

SYRISCOS: Well, that's up to you –
Do as you like; but if you're making all this fuss
Hoping I'll give you a little something for yourself
In exchange for the ring, you're barmy. I'm not going shares,
Not on your life.

ONESIMOS: I didn't ask for anything.

SYRISCOS: Look – I must run; I've several things to do in
town.
I'll soon be back; we'll see then what seems best to do.

[SYRISCOS *goes off towards Athens.* HABROTONON
comes up to Onesimos.]

HABROTONON: Onesimos! This baby the woman's nursing
now
Indoors – was it the charcoal-burner who found it?

ONESIMOS: Yes,
He says so.

HABROTONON: Poor little mite, it's very sweet.

ONESIMOS: What's more,
This ring was on the child; and – it's my master's ring.

HABROTONON: Well, then, if he's in fact your master's son,
you couldn't
Surely stand by and see him brought up as a slave?
Why, that's as bad as murder!

ONESIMOS: I was just telling you,
No one knows who the mother is.

HABROTONON: He lost the ring,
You say, at the Tauropolia?

ONESIMOS: Yes; he was drunk, or so
The boy attending him told me.

HABROTONON [*reflectively*]: He'd be alone, of course,
When he came across the women dancing at dead of night.
– Why, just such a thing happened under my very eyes!

ONESIMOS: Under your . . .?

HABROTONON: Yes, at last year's Tauropolia.
  I was there to play for the dances. There was this young girl
  Dancing with all the rest – it never occurred to me
  At the time; I didn't know then about men, you see –
  That's true, by Aphrodite.

ONESIMOS: Well, who was this girl?
  Do you know?

HABROTONON: No, but I could find out. She was a friend
  Of the women I was with.

ONESIMOS: Did you catch her father's name?

HABROTONON: Nothing; but I would know her if I saw her
    again.
  She was simply lovely; and they mentioned she was rich.

ONESIMOS: It might be her.

HABROTONON: I don't know. While she was
    there with us
  She wandered off; then suddenly came running back
  Alone and sobbing, tearing her hair; her pretty dress
  Of finest Tarantine silk all ruined, torn to shreds.

ONESMIOS: Did she have this ring?

HABROTONON: Perhaps; she didn't show it me,
  To be quite truthful.

ONESIMOS: Well, then, what must I do now?

HABROTONON: Look here, if you'll be sensible and listen to
    me,
  Go to your master; lay all the facts in front of him.
  Suppose this child's the son of a free-born girl; then why
  Should not Charisios know what happened?

ONESIMOS: Yes – but first
  Let's find out who the girl is; that's where you come in.
  Now, think . . .

HABROTONON: Oh, no, I couldn't; not until I know
  For certain who the man is who assaulted her.
  What frightens me is the thought of giving a false lead

To the women I told you of. Who knows? Some other man
May have happened to lay a bet with him and win the ring
And then lose it again at dice. Or he paid it down,
Perhaps, as earnest of his share in a Club dinner.
Or else he made some agreement, and handed over the ring
To get himself out of a tight corner. A thing like that,
Once men get drinking, can easily happen a thousand ways.
Until I know the guilty man, I don't intend
To look for the girl, or breathe a word to anyone.

ONESIMOS: That's not a bad bit of reasoning. Well, what shall
we do?

HABROTONON: I've thought of a plan, Onesimos; see what
you think of it.
It's this: I will pretend the whole thing happened to me.
I'll take this ring, and go in and see Charisios.

ONESIMOS: Yes, go on.

HABROTONON: When he sees I've got the ring he'll ask
Where I got it from. I'll say, 'At the Tauropolia,
When I was still a virgin' – and I'll tell everything
As my own story; I know the details well enough.

ONESIMOS: A first-rate scheme.

HABROTONON: You'll see, if he's the guilty man,
He'll rush head-over-heels to give himself away.
He's drunk now; so he'll pour out everything at once.
I'll let *him* mention details first, rather than me,
And agree to what he says; I mustn't make any slips.

ONESIMOS: Magnificent!

HABROTONON: To make sure I don't get anything
wrong
I'll bluff it out with the usual phrases – 'What a brute
You were to me; nothing would stop you!'

ONESIMOS: That's the stuff!

HABROTONON: 'You were so rough,' I'll say, 'throwing me
to the ground,
Tearing my lovely dress to bits!' But first I'll go

And see the woman who has the baby; I'll pick it up,
And cry, and kiss it, and ask her where she got it from.

ONESIMOS: You're wonderful!

HABROTONON: Then for the final stroke I'll show
This foundling; and I'll tell him, 'There's your baby son!'

ONESIMOS: Perfect, my duck; wickedly clever!

HABROTONON: And if then
It all comes clear, and he's proved father of the child,
We'll take our time to find the girl.

ONESIMOS: There's one thing more
You haven't mentioned: you'll be set free! Once he thinks
You're his son's mother, he'll buy your freedom on the
spot.

HABROTONON: I don't know. Oh, if only . . . !

ONESIMOS: You don't know? You do!
And by the way, who will you have to thank? Why, me!

HABROTONON: Why, heavens, yes! For everything! I don't
know what
I'd have done without you!

ONESIMOS: Now, if you just give up the idea
Of finding the girl – just drop the matter, and let me
down,
What happens then?

HABROTONON: Stupid! Why should I? Do you imagine
I dote on babies? All I want is to be free.
Gods, give me that for my reward!

ONESIMOS: I pray they will.

HABROTONON: Agreed, then?

ONESIMOS: Absolutely. If you play tricks on me –
I'll fight you *then* – I'll have a hold on you. Meanwhile
Let's see how this plan goes.

HABROTONON: You agree then?

ONESIMOS: Certainly.

HABROTONON: Quick, then, give me the ring.

ONESIMOS [*handing the ring*]:   Take it.

HABROTONON: Dear goddess, hear!
    Holy Persuasion, help me! Bring my words success!
        [*Exit* HABROTONON *into Chaerestratos' house.*]
ONESIMOS [*alone*]: I call that smart! Our little girl no sooner
        sees
    That the trade of love's a blind alley, and not the road
    That leads to freedom, than she tries the other tack.
    But look at me: I'll be a slave my whole life long,
    A snivelling booby – never a thought to better myself.
    However, if she's lucky, perhaps I'll get a share –
    It's only right – Pah! That way of reckoning makes no
        sense;
    I'm a poor fool, to hope for gratitude from a woman.
    I only pray not to be worse off than before.
    My mistress, now, Charisios' wife – things might well
        take
    A nasty turn for her, and soon. Suppose this girl,
    The mother of this infant, should turn out to be
    A free man's daughter: then Charisios will take
    Her, and get rid of Pamphile his present wife.
    For the moment, though, I think I've neatly dodged the
        blame
    For stirring up this present trouble. For the future –
    I've done with meddling, thank you. If anyone catches me
    Minding what's not my business, or speaking out of turn
    Ever again, he's welcome to cut off both my – ears.
        [*He sees Smicrines coming back from Athens.*]
    Now who can this be? Smicrines, on his way back
    From town – and once again all wound up for a row.
    Has someone told him the real reason for the quarrel
    Between his daughter and my master? I'd rather keep
    Out of the way. It's quite possible, I should think,
    He's coming to fetch his daughter home. And *my* cue is –
    Let well alone.
        [*Exit* ONESIMOS. *Enter* SMICRINES.]

At this point a further considerable portion of the play is lost, or survives only in tattered papyri where one or two words at the beginning or end of a line are legible. From these remains a certain amount of conjecture is possible. Smicrines on reaching the stage addresses the audience somewhat as follows:

SMICRINES: I was deceived in that young man Charisios. He is nothing but a profligate. The whole town talks of his scandalous behaviour. It's clear that he's a bad character; he drinks all day, and disgraces his name by the life he leads. And now, I learn, for more than three days he has been living apart from his wife, my daughter. I thought at first I would try to reconcile them; but now, it seems, he has taken a guitar-girl to live with him. This, on top of drinking and gambling, is too much; I've done with patience!

Next, a Cook arrives, probably a similar character to the Cook in *The Bad-Tempered Man*. He has been sent for by Charisios to prepare an extravagant banquet for him and his friends. The sight of such preparations increases the rage of Smicrines at his son-in-law's behaviour. Later Simmias, a friend of Charisios, is on the stage, and a line addressed to him suggests that Habrotonon has succeeded in her interview with Charisios, and that he has now acknowledged the child as hers and his. Smicrines, as always, is the last person to find out what is going on.

SMICRINES: The beggar drinks only the most expensive
    wine.
  That's what puts *me* in a rage. I don't say a word about
  Just getting drunk – which after all's plain greediness,
  Even if you make yourself swill down the twopenny stuff;
  But this is the last straw – he's going to throw to the winds
  His whole fortune! What's that to do with me, you say?
  I tell you once more, he'll be sorry! Four talents
  Of silver my daughter brought him as her dowry; yet
  He's made his mind up not to be his wife's footman.

He sleeps away from home. He pays a pimp three pounds
Per day for a whore, three pounds! He has a marvellous
    head
For business, has Charisios. Now tell me: what sum
Is reckoned enough to keep a man, humanely speaking?
Two shillings a day. – Well, where on earth's the sense in
    paying
More to a hungry man?

      [*Enter* CHAERESTRATOS *with* ONESIMOS. SMI-
      CRINES *at first does not notice them.*]

ONESIMOS: Chaerestratos, I see someone on the look-out for
    you.
CHAERESTRATOS: This man? Bless you, who is he?
ONESIMOS: Your son's father-in-law,
    Raging and cursing at his miserable luck.
SMICRINES: She's pretty, it seems, this guitar-girl he's
    acquired; and so
    This graceless, brainless, heartless son-in-law of mine
    Decides to abandon his devoted, faithful wife . . .

A gap here of some fifteen lines, in which Chaerestratos tries to put
in a plea for his son.

CHAERESTRATOS: . . . So pause, my friend, I beg you, as you
    hope for luck.
SMICRINES: You just keep quiet. You go to hell. You'll
    regret this.
    I'm going indoors now; and when I've found out exactly
    How things are with my daughter, I must then decide
    On the best way of dealing with Charisios.
      [*Exit* SMICRINES *into Charisios' house.*]
ONESIMOS: Ought we to warn Charisios that the old man's
    here?
CHAERESTRATOS: Oh, the young monkey! Turning his
    whole house upside down!

ONESIMOS: I wish he'd turned some others upside down.

CHAERESTRATOS: What others?

ONESIMOS: Next door, for one.

CHAERESTRATOS: *My* house?

ONESIMOS: Yes, yours. Let's go in now
  And see Charisios.

CHAERESTRATOS: Yes, let's go; here comes a crowd
  Of rowdy youths, half soaked. It seems a good idea
  To keep out of their way.
        [*They both go in.*]

The last five lines above are puzzling. They seem to suggest that
the house of Chaerestratos, where Charisios has been living with
Habrotonon, is in fact under lease to Habrotonon's owner, the pimp,
who has accepted Charisios as a tenant as long as Charisios is paying
for Habrotonon. This raises the question, Why didn't Chaerestratos
let his house to his son who was getting married, instead of to a
pimp? Was it accepted that a respectable man might let his property
for a brothel? These are some of the unanswered questions in an
incomplete play.

Act 4

Enter ONESIMOS *alone.*

ONESIMOS: Human life is all peril and uncertainty.
Look at me: what's my city? my safeguard? my law?
My one judge of all right or wrong? My master is
All these to me. At his sole pleasure I must live.
But that old Smicrines, damn him – without a thought for
us . . .

Of the next few scenes only a few lines survive, mostly from
quotations. The next fragment is in the latter part of Act 4, and
discovers Pamphile in conversation with her father Smicrines.

PAMPHILE: . . . But if, while saving me from my husband,
you should fail
To convince me this is best, it would be clear that you
Are not my father but my master now.
SMICRINES [*indignantly*]: Hear that!
That's Pamphile giving utterance! Shouting that she wants
Reason, persuasion, no compulsion! But if I
May be allowed a word, I'd like to make three points
For your reflection. First, your marriage has now reached
A state where there's no hope for either him or you.
He'll go on living in this wild fashion, enjoying himself.
You won't enjoy yourself one bit. Even suppose
You live in his house, will he let you have a servant-girl
If you happen to need one? One of his visiting tarts,
perhaps?
Not likely! Husband first in everything, that's the rule;
Wife nowhere.

After a gap of about twenty-four lines Smicrines is again – or still –
speaking.

And then, see how expensive it's going to be for him,
At festival-time, Pamphile. He'll have to buy
Two tickets for Thesmophoria; *two* tickets again
For Scirophoria – think of the financial strain!
Why, he's as good as bankrupt, never a doubt of it.
Picture what sort of a life *you*'ll have. 'I must be off,'
Says your husband, 'to Peiraeus.' He goes; does duty there.
Not pleasant for you? Just wait. He's back again in Athens –
Drinking, of course, with a whore –

PAMPHILE: I think I'll be going now;
Someone's come out . . .

A gap of perhaps seventy lines, during which this Scene ends and the
next Scene begins.[1] The new Scene probably opened with a soliloquy
by Habrotonon telling how, as a result of her pretence, Charisios
has acknowledged his lustful act at the Tauropolia, and believes
the child to be his and Habrotonon its mother. So now it remains
for Habrotonon to find the real mother; and she will begin by making
enquiries of the women who hired her to play on that occasion.

When she has finished, Sophrone, Pamphile's old nurse, comes
with Pamphile to the door of Charisios' house. Habrotonon recognizes Pamphile, who then goes in, while Sophrone comes forward
on the stage. During Sophrone's first lines Habrotonon slips back
into the house and quickly comes out again with the baby. Then she
listens, concealed in the doorway, to what Sophrone is saying, which
(though only five lines survive) would probably include words to
make it even clearer to Habrotonon that Pamphile is the mother of
the child. Sophrone describes the arguments which Smicrines has
been using to persuade Pamphile to leave Charisios and return home.

SOPHRONE: My eyes are all burnt up, I've cried so much
today.
I'll tell you what her father Smicrines said to her.
'Pamphile,' he said, 'for a free-born woman to fight a
whore

1. I have followed E. Capps's reconstruction.

Is courting trouble. A whore's much more unscrupulous,
More knowing; ashamed of nothing; a better wheedler
  too . . .'

> [HABROTONON *comes forward holding the child, who is crying. At first she speaks only to herself or the child.*]

HABROTONON: I'll take baby for a walk. Poor mite, he will
  cry so!
I've had him poorly now for days and days. There, there!
SOPHRONE [*to herself*]: I don't know what to do. If only the
  gods would help!
HABROTONON [*to the baby*]: Poor darling, I'm so sorry for
  you. We'll go out.
I don't know what to do; but all the same we'll go.
[*To Sophrone*]: Excuse me! Wait for me one moment.

> [HABROTONON *now sees Sophrone's face, and recognizes her as having been with Pamphile at the Tauropolia.*]

                                        I'm so glad
I've found you!
SOPHRONE: Found me? Why, then, who do you think I am?
HABROTONON [*to herself*]: It is! I recognize her. [*To
  Sophrone*] Glad to see you again!
Bless you, turn round and look, now! Listen to me a
  minute.
SOPHRONE: Look here, what are you talking about?
HABROTONON: A year ago
At the Tauropolia I saw you, if I'm not mistaken.

> [*Now Sophrone has seen the tokens hung round the child's neck.*]

SOPHRONE: Tell me – this baby of yours – where did you
  get him from?
HABROTONON: Oh, bless you, bless you! You see something you recognize?
Yes, how did he get this? – Please don't be afraid of me.

SOPHRONE: Then you are not its mother?

HABROTONON: I pretended to be;
Not so as to steal him from her, but to give me time
To find out who she is. And now I've found – well –
you.
You're the same person I saw then.

SOPHRONE: But who's his father?

HABROTONON: Charisios!

SOPHRONE: My dear girl, are you sure of that?

HABROTONON [showing the ring]: Do you know this ring? Is
it the property of the man
Whose young wife I've just seen indoors?

SOPHRONE: Why, yes, it is!

HABROTONON: The gods must love you! You asked for
help, and here it is.
One of your neighbours is coming out; I heard the door.
Come, take me in with you to your mistress's house;
Then I can tell you the whole story, end to end.

> [*They both go into Charisios' house. Out of Chaerestratos' house comes* ONESIMOS; *as he speaks he points behind him into the house.*]

ONESIMOS: This man's going slightly mad. He *is* mad, by
Apollo.
He's really gone mad, by all the gods. In fact – he's mad.
I allude to my master, Charisios; he's suffering
From neurotic paranoia – something of that sort.
That's only a guess; but what else could it be? Just now
For half an hour he was bending down and listening
At the door of the other house, where his wife's father, it
seems,
Was urging her to leave her husband. Charisios
Turned pale, then red – I really shouldn't give him away.
He was calling aloud, 'Darling, what noble words you
speak!'
Then he beat his head with clenched fists; and after a while

He began again: 'What a wonderful wife I've got,' says he;
'And what a wonderful, miserable mess I've made of
    things!'
At last, when he'd heard everything, he came indoors;
And there he was in his room, groaning, tearing his hair,
Raving incessantly. 'Yes, I'm a criminal,' he'd say
Again and again. 'After myself doing what I did,
And being myself the father of a bastard child,
I was such a brute and savage that I neither felt,
Nor offered her, one shred of forgiveness – although she
Had suffered the very wrong that I was guilty of.'
He loads himself with reproaches, rages at himself
With bloodshot eyes. I'm terrified; my mouth's all dry.
If while he's in this state he catches sight of *me*,
The one who told him his wife's trouble, like as not
He'd kill me. That's why I've slipped out here. What can I
    do?
Where can I go? I'm finished, done for. – That's the
    door;
He's coming out. – O Saviour Zeus, if possible
Save me!
        [*Enter from the house* CHARISIOS; ONESIMOS *remains
        at first unseen.*]
CHARISIOS: I was the faultless man who made honour my
    aim;
I the student of ethics, sifting right from wrong;
My life immaculate, blameless! Now my own folly
Has shown my feet of clay; and the just gods have sent
My fit reward. 'You poor wretch, all conceit and talk,'
I hear them say, 'You reject your wife for a mishap
That was forced upon her; now we'll show the world that
    you
Tripped up on the same wire. And when it all comes out
She'll use you gently – you who now dishonour her.
Then you'll be known as an example to the world –

Not of bad luck, but of sheer crass brutality.
Compare what *she* said to her father, with what *you*
Were thinking about her. "I came to share his life" –
That's what she said – "so certainly I must not try
To step aside from this mischance that's come to me."
But you – you self-conceited prig! – how different
Was your behaviour!'

The next twenty lines of the text are fragmentary, and the translation largely conjectural. Habrotonon enters at some point.

                        Now her father Smicrines
Will think the worst, and treat her as she has not deserved.
Well, what do I care for Smicrines? I'll tell him off!
'Look here,' I'll say to him, 'just you stop making trouble
And pestering Pamphile. My wife's not leaving me!'
      [*He sees Onesimos.*]
What, are you here again?

ONESIMOS [*aside to Habrotonon*]: Things look pretty black to me.
For God's sake don't desert me.

CHARISIOS: You there! You blackmailer!
Are you eavesdropping?

ONESIMOS: By all the gods, I've just come out.

CHARISIOS: You louse, last time you eavesdropped, no good came of it.

ONESIMOS: Why, when do you mean, sir? Where, sir? I assure you, sir –

CHARISIOS: Still jabbering, are you? Right, take that! [*He hits him.*]

ONESIMOS: Oh! – Nothing, sir!
You're doing me a wrong, though, master; you'll soon see.

CHARISIOS: I'll teach you a lesson soon enough.

HABROTONON [*coming forward*]:   Charisios!
    There's something you don't know yet.

CHARISIOS: Something I don't know?

HABROTONON: That child I showed you wasn't mine. I made
    that up.

CHARISIOS: Not yours? Whose then? Quick, tell me.

HABROTONON: Will you set me free
    If I tell you?

CHARISIOS: I'll see you whipped and hanged if you don't
    tell me
    This instant.

HABROTONON: Yes, I'd better tell. That child's your wife's.

CHARISIOS: Are you quite sure?

HABROTONON: Quite sure. Speak up, Onesimos.

CHARISIOS [*to Onesimos*]: Well, what about it? Are you two
    just trying me out?

ONESIMOS: *She* put me up to it, by Apollo I swear she did.

CHARISIOS: You'll twist me round, will you, you little
    twister, you?

HABROTONON: Now, dear Charisios, have it out with me.
    This child
    Is your own wedded wife's and no one else's.

CHARISIOS: Oh!
    I wish it were!

HABROTONON: It is, by the dear goddess.

CHARISIOS: But –
    How can I believe such a thing?

HABROTONON: It's true!

CHARISIOS: You mean, this child
    Is really Pamphile's child?

HABROTONON: Yes, her child – and yours too.

CHARISIOS: Pamphile's child? For God's sake, girl, don't
    lead me on
    With false hope.

HABROTONON: This is true, sir; but I had to wait
  Before explaining, till I was sure of all the facts.

Here there is a gap of several lines, in which presumably Habrotonon
tells how she carried out her plot. Then Charisios goes into his own
house to see Pamphile. End of Act 4.

Act 5
SCENE ONE

CHAERESTRATOS, ONESIMOS.

ONESIMOS: Listen, Chaerestratos. This slave-girl Habro-
tonon –
I'll tell you what she said next. 'Onesimos,' she said,
'It's your duty to stay loyal in all respects –
And you know what I mean – loyal to Charisios.'
There now! She's not your ordinary hired girl! People
Who act like that are not to be met with every day.
It was her determination that found the child for
you.
CHAERESTRATOS: You can have your freedom – it's
sett¹ed. Come, don't hang your head!
And now, first go and find Charisios alone,
My own son, my beloved boy . . .

Another gap; then a fragment which probably belongs here.

CHAERESTRATOS: You never could mind your own
business, Onesimos;
But I love you all the same.
ONESIMOS: There's nothing I love more
Than finding everything out . . .

After another considerable gap we have these lines, probably ending
the scene.

CHAERESTRATOS: . . . I'm sure now Habrotonon's a decent,
virtuous girl.
But – how attractive she is! I know Charisios:

137

He'd never have kept his hands off, if she hadn't been
The soul of virtue. Well, I'll keep my hands off too.

[*Exit* CHAERESTRATOS, *perhaps with Habrotonon, to
go to buy her freedom from her owner.*]

SCENE TWO

Enter SMICRINES *alone.*

SMICRINES [*to himself*]: Sophrone, I'm damned if I won't
    split your skull for you!
  You'll give me a piece of your mind, like all the rest, will
    you?
  I'm in too much of a hurry, am I, because I intend
  To take my daughter away – you nagging old rag-bag,
    you?
  Must I stand by and watch this precious son-in-law
  Eat up my money in my daughter's house? Must I
  Argue with you about things which are *my* concern? Is
    that
  What you'd like me to do? Isn't it better to take the bull
  By the horns? Just you say one more word, and see what
    you get!
  Damn it, am I to plead my case before Sophrone?
  I'm to interview that tart and persuade her to go home,
  Am I? I tell you, Sophrone, as I hope to live:
  You've seen that pond by the side of the road on the way
    home?
  I'm going to duck you in it again and again all night
  And drown you dead. I'll teach you to have your own
    opinion
  And take sides against me.
       [*He tries the door of Charisios' house.*]
                  This door seems to be locked;
  All right, I'll bang. [*He bangs on the door.*]
  Hi, you there, slaves! Are you all deaf? Open this door!
      [ONESIMOS *opens it and stands firmly in the doorway.*]
ONESIMOS: Who's that knocking at the door? Oh, is it
  Smicrines,

139

Old Pepper-pot, come to fetch his dowry and his daughter?

SMICRINES: You know who I am, blast your eyes.

ONESIMOS: Quite right, quite right!
A very rational, sensible intention too:
A real, first-class abduction.

SMICRINES: Oh! You immortal gods!

ONESIMOS: Smicrines, do you imagine the immortal gods
Have so little to do that they can spend their days
Dealing out good and bad to individuals?

SMICRINES: What do you mean?

ONESIMOS: I'll put it simply for you. How many
Cities are there in the whole world? Let's say a thousand.
In each of them three hundred thousand people live.
Do the gods punish or reward each one of them
Separately? That's not how the gods live! The gods
Are at peace. A life like that would be one endless head-
ache!
You'll ask me, Don't the gods then care about us at all?
They do. They assign to each man his appropriate
Character, to command the garrison of his soul.
This inner force drives one man straight to ruin, if ever
He has abused it; leads another to happiness.
Character is our god, which apportions to each man
Good luck or bad. Propitiate this god, by acting
Kindly and decently; and deserve a happy life.

SMICRINES: You snivelling scab! Don't I act decently?
What's wrong
With *my* character, then?

ONESIMOS: It's driving you to ruin.

SMICRINES: Confound your impudence!

ONESIMOS: Smicrines, do you consider
It right for a man to take his daughter from her husband?

SMICRINES: Right? No one says it's right; but in this case it's
necessary.

ONESIMOS [*appealing to audience*]: You see? This chap
  reckons what's wrong is necessary!
  It's not his character letting him down; it's something else.
     [*He taps his forehead.*]
  Only just now you were set on doing a wicked thing;
  And what has saved you? Just the natural course of events.
  Result: all difficulties smoothed away and solved.
  So, Smicrines, don't let me catch you another time
  Acting precipitately; I warn you. For the present
  Consider yourself acquitted on these charges. Now,
  Go in, pick up your grandson and pay your respects to
    him.

SMICRINES: My *grandson*? What do you mean? You're only
  fit for flogging!

ONESIMOS: You've got a thick skin too, Dad – and a thicker
  skull.
  Your marriageable daughter – is that how you took care of
    her?
  So, five-months children are born; we rear them! Miracle!

SMICRINES: I haven't the slightest idea what you're talking
  about.

ONESIMOS: Maybe;
  But I think old Sophrone has. On a certain date my
    master –
  In fact, at last year's Tauropolia –

SMICRINES [*shouting in at the door*]: Sophrone!

ONESIMOS: – my master found your daughter, dragged her
  off by force
  From where the rest were dancing – there you are, you
    see!

SMICRINES: I see.

ONESIMOS: Now he and she have recognized each other;
  And all is bliss.
     [SOPHRONE *has now entered.*]

SMICRINES: Come here, you pocket-picking hag.

141

Just tell me what he's talk'ng about.

SOPHRONE [*striking an attitude*]:   ''Twas Nature's will,
Who respects not man's law. For this was woman born.'

SMICRINES: Have you gone mad?

SOPHRONE: I'll say the whole speech, end to end,
If you still can't put two and two together, Smicrines.
It's from Euripides' *Auge*.

SMICRINES: Oh, you make me sick,
Reciting poetry. Well you know it's preposterous,
What Onesimos said.

SOPHRONE: I know; there were two preposterous things—
And he's made sense of both of them.

SMICRINES [*as understanding glimmers*]: Why, bless my soul!
But this is extraordinary!

SOPHRONE: It's the most wonderful piece of luck
There ever was.

SMICRINES: If what you're saying's really true,
Why, then, this child is . . .!

PERICEIROMENE
OR
THE UNKINDEST CUT

CHARACTERS

POLEMON, *a Corinthian soldier*
GLYCERA, *his mistress*
SOSIAS, *Polemon's slave*
DORIS, *Glycera's maid*
The goddess IGNORANCE, *or Imperfect Knowledge*
DAOS, *Moschion's slave*
PATAICOS, *a Corinthian merchant*
MYRRHINE, *a wealthy Corinthian woman*
MOSCHION, *son of Myrrhine*
HABROTONON, *a guitar-girl*
CHORUS *of tipsy guests*

*

Scene: A street in Corinth. There are three houses, belonging respectively to Polemon, Pataicos and Myrrhine.

Act 1

SCENE ONE

Almost the whole of the first scene is missing. The following is a conjectural summary:

Glycera lives in the house of her lover Polemon, who is away on military service. Moschion, the son of her neighbour Myrrhine, sees her at her door, comes up to her, and embraces and kisses her. She does not protest or resist. At that moment Sosias arrives to announce that Polemon is back from the war and will soon reach his home. Sosias interrupts Glycera's encounter with Moschion; Moschion vanishes, and Sosias goes off to tell Polemon what he has seen. Polemon arrives and challenges Glycera; she does not deny the fact, and is hesitant in her answers. Polemon, convinced of her infidelity, storms at her. She runs into the house; Polemon follows her, and there in his rage cuts off her hair. Then Glycera reappears shorn and weeping, followed by Polemon full of remorse and guilt and baffled jealousy. Of this scene only three lines survive.

POLEMON: Don't cry, Glycera! I swear to you by Olympian
  Zeus
  And by Athene – dearest, dearest Glycera –!
GLYCERA: I've heard you swear you love me a thousand
  times already!

After this, Polemon in despair goes into the house of his friend and neighbour Pataicos. Glycera and her maid Doris discuss what is to be done. Glycera says she is too much afraid of Polemon to stay in his house. She returns there to pack her belongings.

SCENE TWO

The next scene opens with the appearance of the goddess Ignorance.
A dozen lines are lost from the beginning of her speech. She tells how,
many years ago, Pataicos' wife had twin children, a boy and a girl;
and how she died soon after their birth. Pataicos at about the same
time lost all his fortune; and feeling unequal to the burden of bringing
up two children, decided to expose them. A poor woman found
them and took them home. Here the MS begins.

IGNORANCE: ... One of these infants, the girl, she resolved
    to keep
And love as her own child; the other she would give
To a wealthy woman who was longing for a baby,
Who lives here in this house.
        [*She points to Myrrhine's house.*]
                        So that was what she did.
Eighteen years passed. War came; and times grew worse
    and worse
For Corinth; and the old woman was at her wits' end.
The child had grown into the girl you saw just now.
She had a lover – that impetuous young man;
So, since he was a Corinthian, she gave the girl,
As if she were giving her own daughter, to this man,
But not in formal marriage. She herself, worn out
With age, remembering that chance might take her off
At any moment, did not hide the truth, but told
The girl how she was found and reared; gave her the
    clothes
She had been wrapped in; also, reflecting how uncertain
All human fortune is, in case the girl should ever
Be in need of help, she told her who her brother was –
Brother by birth, though no one knew it. For she saw,
First, that he was the only relative she had;
And next, she thought it wise to safeguard both of them

From unwitting involvement, which might well result
From me – that is, from Ignorance. She knew this boy
Was rich, and always getting drunk; the girl was young
And pretty, and now was being left in a position
That was anything but stable. So the old woman died.
The soldier Polemon, the girl's lover, bought this house
Not long ago; and she, living next door to her brother,
Has breathed no word of what she knows; nor does she
    want
To endanger the distinguished social rank which now
Seems to be his: what Fortune has given him, she feels,
He should enjoy.
                        Now, yesterday evening, quite by chance –
I told you he's a lively, aggressive lad, and always
Hanging around the house – he just caught sight of her
When she was sending her servant on some errand. As
    soon
As he saw her there at the door, he ran across and
    began
Kissing and hugging her. She, knowing he was her
    brother,
Did not run away. That moment, up comes Sosias
And sees them. Well, it's easy to guess what happened
    then.
He went off saying he'd ask her at the proper time
What she meant by it. She stood there crying, heart-
    broken that
She was not free to embrace and kiss her own brother.

And all this flared up for the sake of what should follow:
First, to set Polemon in a rage – by nature he's not
That sort of person; it was I leading him on
To set in motion the whole train of discoveries,
And so that both may at last find their families
And be re-united with them. So, if any of you

Were shocked at what happened and thought it terrible,
   think again.
Evil itself, in the very act, swings round to good
Under Heaven's guiding hand. So, ladies and gentlemen,
Good-bye! Be kind; and give the rest of the play success!

SCENE THREE

Enter SOSIAS *from Pataicos' house.*

SOSIAS: Polemon, our violent warrior of an hour ago,
    Polemon, who says women are not to keep their hair –
    Is sitting at table, crying. I've just left him there
    At lunch with the whole household; and his friends have
      come
    In a body to persuade him not to take it all
    So much to heart. Since he's no way of finding out
    What's going on here [*he points to Polemon's house*] he sends
      me to fetch his cloak.
    He doesn't want his cloak; it's just his whim to keep
    Me on the run.
           [DORIS *appears with* GLYCERA *at the door of Polemon's*
           house; when Doris comes out, Glycera disappears in-
           doors. SOSIAS *stands at one side, and Doris does not see*
           him.]
DORIS: Yes, madam, I'll just go and see.
SOSIAS [*aside*]: That's Doris. How she's grown up! There's a
    lovely wench!
    Well! These Corinthian dames live in some style, I see.
    Now, in we go.
           [DORIS *goes across to Myrrhine's door;* SOSIAS, *unseen*
           by her, slips into Polemon's house.]
DORIS: I'll knock at Myrrhine's door. There's no one
    About out here. [*She knocks.*] I'm sorry for any girl who
      has
    A soldier for a husband. They're a lawless lot;
    You just can't trust them. The way he's treated Glycera –
    It's so outrageous! [*She knocks again.*] Hullo, there!
           [*While Doris is intent on Myrrhine's door,* SOSIAS *slips*
           out of Polemon's house.]

SOSIAS: Polemon will be pleased
    To hear she's crying at this moment – the very thing
    He wanted.

       [SOSIAS *goes into Pataicos' house. A slave-boy opens*
       Myrrhine's door to Doris.]

DORIS: Ask your mistress, sonny, to come out here.

At this point about seventy lines are missing, during which, it would
seem, Myrrhine comes out, and Glycera comes out of Polemon's
house; and it is arranged that Glycera shall move into Myrrhine's
house for the present. Myrrhine's slave Daos, with some others,
carries Glycera's luggage across – only a few belongings, since most
of her dresses, as we find later, are left in Polemon's house. Probably
in this scene Glycera tells Myrrhine that she is Moschion's sister, and
mentions as proof the ornaments which were left with her when she
was exposed. Myrrhine has always pretended, even to her husband,
that Moschion was her own child.

      [*When Glycera has gone indoors with Myrrhine,* DAOS
      sees Polemon's tipsy guests coming out of Pataicos' house,
      and hurries his fellow-slaves into Myrrhine's house.]

DAOS: Come on, hurry up now! There's a great gang of lads
    coming,
    All drunk. [*To the audience*] I give my mistress full marks;
        she's invited
    Glycera in on purpose. There's a mother for you!
    I must fetch my young master; if I'm not mistaken,
    This is the moment for him to come home double-quick!
      [*Exit* DAOS.]

Act 2

SCENE ONE

MOSCHION *and* DAOS *enter from the town.*

MOSCHION: Daos, you rat, many a time you've told me lies.
   You bare-faced crook!
   Are you once more leading me up the garden? Because if
   you are –
DAOS: If I am, just get a rope and hang me now.
MOSCHION: Say that again.
DAOS: Treat me as you would your enemy. But, if what I've
   said is true,
   If you find her there indoors now, Moschion – if you now
   possess
   All you've been pursuing, if *my* endless arguments induced
   Her to come here, and your mother to receive her, and
   provide
   Everything your heart could wish for: what's *my* future, if
   you please?
MOSCHION:[1] What's your future, Daos? Just think – what
   would please you most of all?
   Come, now, what do you really long for? Isn't the treadmill your first choice?
DAOS: Send me to the treadmill, do – if Polemon doesn't get
   here first.
   Then the wooden collar will soon be clapped on someone
   else's neck.
MOSCHION [*coaxing*]: Look here, Daos: I want to make you
   steward-in-chief of my affairs,
   Major-domo, generalissimo, Daos! Now, don't let me
   down!

   1. The MS here is badly damaged, and the next twenty lines are largely
conjecture.

DAOS: Well, the blockade's not begun yet; you've still time
to run indoors.

MOSCHION: But – suppose, now, you betrayed me – sold me
out to Polemon?

DAOS: Look – I'll need some gold – say seven talents –

MOSCHION: Is there anything
You wouldn't do for money?

DAOS: Moschion, let's be realistic now.
I've been shopping.

[He taps a large bag which he is carrying.]

Plenty of food here. The plain truth is, we're at war.
Right – then let me plan the strategy. Spend twelve talents,
if need be,

Straight off, rather than be made a fool of. Doesn't that
make sense?

MOSCHION: Tell that to the washer-women, corner-boy!

DAOS: Look – there's a chance
Seven talents may buy off Polemon. Shall I try it?

MOSCHION: Name of Zeus!
You're no general – you're a fried-fish cheap-jack. I'll see
you in jail.

DAOS: Is this meant to win my loyal service, master – talk
like this?

Waste no more time; get indoors now.

MOSCHION: I'd best leave it all to you.
Talk them over if you can, then. If you can't, I'll have to
come

Out and fight this goddam feather-crested brigadier.

DAOS: You will.

MOSCHION: Wait, though, Daos – you go in first. Find out
how the land lies there.

See what Glycera's doing; where my mother is; whether
they feel

Welcoming towards me. I don't need to tell you what to
do,

Do I? You've got your head screwed on.

DAOS: I'll go.

MOSCHION: I'll just walk up and down
   Here by the door and wait for you.

         [DAOS *goes into the house.*]

                     Last night when I went up to her
   She showed clearly how she felt towards me; didn't run
      away;
   Put her arms right round me, held me tight. Well, by
      Athene! I'm
   Not bad-looking; quite good company; girls are apt to
      fall for me.
   This is a critical moment; I'd be wise to say a prayer for
      luck.

         [DAOS *comes out again.*]

DAOS: Moschion! She's had her bath. She's sitting down now.

MOSCHION: Darling girl!

DAOS: Your Mamma's just pottering round with this and
   that. The midday meal's
   Ready. From the look of things I'd say they were expect-
      ing you.

MOSCHION: They've been waiting too long. Who says I'm
   not handsome? – Did you say
   I was here?

DAOS: No.

MOSCHION: Go and tell them.

DAOS [*dashing off*]:   I'll be back in just two ticks.

MOSCHION [*alone*]: If she feels too shy to tell me that she
   loves me – well, I'll just
   Question her, call Daos as witness. – Wait: as soon as I go
      in,
   First I'd better kiss my mother, get her firmly on my
      side,
   Be as sweet as possible to her, be her own and only boy.
   After all, she's shown a personal interest in this affair.

I hear someone coming out.

    [DAOS *appears, looking glum.*]

                Well, what's wrong, Daos? Why, you seem
Quite reluctant to come near me.

DAOS: So I am, by Zeus – What's wrong?
Everything. When I went in and told your mother you
    were here,
'That's enough of that,' says she; 'now how does Moschion
    know of this?
Did *you* tell him Glycera was frightened and took refuge
    here?
Out of my sight, blast you,' says she, 'crawl away and
    drown yourself.'
That's the truth, then: once they knew that you were
    waiting here to pounce,
Psst! your prize was whisked away.

MOSCHION: You skunk! You dare to laugh at me?

DAOS: Laughing, am I? Ask your mother –!

MOSCHION: What about her? Did she bring
Glycera here against her will, then? Wasn't this plan set on
    foot
Just for my sake? You said you persuaded her to come to
    me!

DAOS: I said I persuaded her? By Apollo, I said no such
    thing!

MOSCHION: Don't think I don't know what lies you're
    telling; since you also said –
Half a minute ago – you'd got my mother to take in
    Glycera
All for my sake!

DAOS: Well – why, yes! I said that. I remember now.

MOSCHION: *And* you said you thought my mother did this in
    my interest.

DAOS: Oh, I can't be sure of that; but I did try persuading
    her.

MOSCHION: Come here. Nearer.

DAOS: How near?

[MOSCHION *hits him.*]

MOSCHION: Do you still think lying pays, you rat?

DAOS: Well, sir, no, sir. Tell the truth, sir – Yes, you're
right, sir; I'm a rat.

MOSCHION: You're being funny with me.

DAOS: No, sir! Cross my heart, sir! Listen, sir:
Probably she doesn't care for doing things in a rush like
that,

On the spur of the moment. She'd prefer to get to know
you first,

Listen to what you've got to say. Remember, she's not
here on hire

Like a flute-girl or some measly prostitute.

MOSCHION: It seems to me,
Daos, you've got a point there.

DAOS: Have I? Test it, then. I'm pretty sure
She's for you. She didn't leave her home, and Polemon,
just for fun.

Hang on here for three or four days. Stick it out. She'll
soon come round.

She, in fact, said just that to me; – may as well tell the
whole truth now.

MOSCHION: Daos, where can I lock you up meanwhile?
You say, just hang on here.

Hang around for three or four days? I'll be hanged to
death by then.

And it's barely ninety seconds since you told me your last
lie!

DAOS: I need time to think, and you keep interrupting. Your
best way,

Master, is to change your tactics. Go in quietly to your
room –

MOSCHION: You'll keep me supplied at meal-times?

DAOS: Look: there's plenty in this bag.
In now, quickly; and lie down. Between us we'll work
something out.

MOSCHION: All right, you can have your way.

[MOSCHION *goes into Myrrhine's house. At the same
time* SOSIAS, *carrying Polemon's cloak and sword, appears
at the door of Pataicos' house just in time to recognize
Moschion. Daos has not yet seen Sosias.*]

DAOS [*mopping his brow*]: A close thing, that, by Heracles!
I'm still trembling; and my tongue's all dry with fright.
I never thought,
When we started, that this kettle of fish would be so hard
to fry.

[SOSIAS *has come downstage to address the audience.*
DAOS *now sees him and stands aside out of sight.*]

SOSIAS: He's sent me back again here with his sword and
cloak;
I'm to find out what Glycera's doing, and bring him
word.
For two pins I'd tell him I found young Moschion
In the house; that'd make him spring to action. But I
won't.
Poor devil, he's had rough luck, and I'm sorry for him.

[*He looks round towards Myrrhine's house.*]

I didn't dream it: that was Moschion all right;
I recognize him from the last time I was here.

[SOSIAS *goes into Polemon's house.* DAOS *comes forward.*]

DAOS: The Foreign Legion's here! This is a pretty mess,
By Apollo, a proper mix-up; and I haven't yet
Thought of the hottest point of all – the flaming row,
The grand bust-up, my master's going to make, if he
Turns up from the country sooner than expected.

[*Polemon's door opens, and* SOSIAS *comes out holding
two slaves by the scruff of the neck.*]

SOSIAS: You!
  You dung-brained oafs, you mules! You've let her go,
    have you?
  You let her through that door, did you? When Polemon
  Gets angry, you'll be lucky if he just cuts your hair!
        [*He turns to the audience.*]
  She's moved across to the neighbour's, to her fancy man;
  And we, says she, can stay here howling till we're hoarse.
        [SOSIAS *walks towards Myrrhine's house.*]

DAOS [*to the audience*]: Listen to Polemon's pet prophet! He's
    not far wrong.

SOSIAS: I'm going to knock at the door. [*He does so.*]

DAOS: Now then, you mangy mongrel, what do you want?
    What's up?

SOSIAS: Are you from that house?

DAOS: Perhaps.

SOSIAS: And you can call *me* names,
  When *you*'re a lot of lunatics! Great gods above!
  You've got some nerve, to take a free-born woman away
  By force from her husband and lock her up.

DAOS: Don't make me sick.
  Whoever you are, you're a blackmailer; sticks out a mile.

SOSIAS: Do you think we in this house have got no guts, no
    fight?
  Are we men, or aren't we?

DAOS: Men? Ha! Twopenny-halfpenny men!
  And when your ninepenny sergeant picks recruits like
    these [*pointing to Sosias' two companions*]
  We'll fight you any minute you like.

SOSIAS: You whipper-snapper!

DAOS: Oh, go to hell! You heard what I said – go to hell.
  You slave of a comic booby! You'll not get hold of her.

SOSIAS: Oh – then you admit you've got her?

DAOS: Do you remember, now –
  Some time ago – oh, I remember! – the way I dealt

With some of your lot?

SOSIAS: Our lot? Who are you talking about?
And who do you think you're being funny with – tell me
that?
You're off your nut. We'll bust your miserable dolls'
house
Wide open in two ticks. Go and help that fancy chap
Buckle his sword on.

DAOS: If this fuss you keep on making
Is all because you think we've got her in *our* house,
You lousy tramp –

SOSIAS: These twopenny-halfpenny men of mine
Will turn you inside out as soon as spit at you.

DAOS: Twopence-halfpenny? I was joking: you're a sewer-
rat,
A dung-worm.

SOSIAS: You be careful, street-boy! I eat flesh.

DAOS: Shog off! [*To the audience*] If he's a man-eater I'm
going indoors.

> [DORIS *has come out of Myrrhine's house in answer to*
> *Sosias' knock.* DAOS *dodges in through the open door.*]

SOSIAS:[1] I warn you, Doris, you've got a lot to answer for;
You're more to blame than anyone else, I tell you
straight.

DORIS: Now, Sosias, be a good fellow and just tell Polemon
That Glycera's gone to stay with a woman friend because
She was frightened.

SOSIAS: Oh, yes! Frightened, was she? Gone to stay
With a woman, has she? Not Myrrhine, by any chance?

DORIS: Just listen, Sosias –

SOSIAS: Gone next door to her fancy man;
To this house, here!

DORIS: You ought to be ashamed of yourself.

---

1. From here to the next gap in the MS the text is largely conjectural.

SOSIAS: Get out of my sight; you're playing a double game,
    I know.

After this comes a gap of more than fifty lines, during which it seems that Polemon plans with Sosias and his other slaves to take Myrrhine's house by storm; while Pataicos, who has been talking to Glycera, tries to persuade Polemon to take a more sober and realistic attitude. With them is the guitar-girl Habrotonon. The following fragments may belong to this part of the play.

PATAICOS: When it's your body that's diseased, you need a
    doctor;
  If it's your mind or heart that's sick, you need a friend.

POLEMON: The only cure for anger is an honest word
  From a good friend.

PATAICOS: However much upset you are,
  Don't let annoyance drive you to act precipitately.
  When things go wrong, a sensible man must above all
  Control unreasoning anger.

POLEMON: Nothing's more welcome than a sympathetic
    friend.

Pataicos' attempts at conciliation are resented by Sosias, who meanwhile has been drinking. The MS resumes.

SOSIAS: You mark my words, he's come here bribed by them
    indoors,
  Myrrhine and Moschion. He's betraying you and your men.
PATAICOS: Look here, my dear chap, give this battle-drill a
    rest;
  Go in and sleep it off. You're not yourself, you know –
  Yes, I mean you; you're drunk, I'll swear.

SOSIAS: What, me? Me drunk?
One little cup I had, or less. I said to myself,
There's trouble coming, I'll keep my head clear, just in case
I'm needed. There you are; that's my luck.

POLEMON [*to Pataicos*]: You're right. – Sosias,
Now listen to me.

SOSIAS [*at attention*]: At your orders, Captain.

POLEMON: That's the style.
Here are your orders. – Habrotonon, give the word of
command.

PATAICOS [*to Polemon*]: First, do tell Sosias and his army to
clear off.

SOSIAS [*to Pataicos*]: You're handling this campaign all wrong.
[*In despair, to audience*] He's making peace,
When he ought to be storming the ramparts.

POLEMON: All my troubles, then,
Come from Pataicos, do they?

SOSIAS [*sulkily*]: He's not general.

HABROTONON: Come on, now, dear man, do go in.

SOSIAS: All right, I'm going.
[*Sosias and his two men go into Polemon's house.*]

POLEMON: I thought you'd manage something, Habrotonon.
You'd be
Useful at a siege yourself, either for straight assault
Or lying covered. – Where are you off to, sweetie-pie?
– Is that tart blushing? – Hey, are you all upset with me?
[*Exit* HABROTONON.]

PATAICOS: Now, Polemon: if the case were such as you
describe,
If someone had seduced your lawful wife –

POLEMON: Lawful?
You know she's not, man. But what difference does it make?
I've always thought of her as my lawful wife.

PATAICOS: Don't shout.
Who gave her to you?

POLEMON: Who gave her? Why, she gave herself.

PATAICOS: That's fair enough. And for a time you pleased
    her. Now
    You don't please her any longer; and since you behaved
    Improperly towards her, she has left you.

POLEMON: What do you mean,
    Improperly? [*Then with a complete change of tone*] In saying
        that you've hit me just
    Where it hurts most.

PATAICOS: You surely must admit that what
    You're doing now is crazy. Just what is your aim?
    To drag her back? She has every right to please herself.
    The one course left for a discontented lover is
    Persuasion.

POLEMON: What of the man who came behind my back
    And seduced her? Isn't he in the wrong?

PATAICOS: He is; and that,
    Should it ever come to a dispute, gives you the right
    To lodge a complaint; but if you take her away by force
    You'll lose your case in a court of law. What he has done
    Gives you the right to sue him, but not to take the law
    Into your own hands.

POLEMON: What? Not even for this?

PATAICOS: Not even
    For this.

POLEMON: I don't know what to say, by God I don't.
    I might as well hang myself. Pataicos, Glycera's left me.
    She's left me, man – Glycera! Look – what do you think?
        Would *you*
    See what you can do? You know her, you've often talked
        with her.
    Be my ambassador; go in and have a word –
    Before I try. Please, now, I beg you.

PATAICOS: A good idea.
    I will.

POLEMON: I suppose you're fairly good at putting a case?

PATAICOS: Fairly.

POLEMON: Oh, but you must be good at it, Pataicos –
  The whole business depends on that. Tell her that I –
  If ever I did her any sort of wrong whatever –
  I swear I love and cherish her every day and hour –
  It's true! – I'd like to show you her dresses –

PATAICOS [*with a deprecating gesture*]:   You're too kind.

POLEMON: Just come and look at them, Pataicos, do. You'll feel
  All the more sorry for me.

PATAICOS: Poseidon!

POLEMON: Come along.
  Marvellous dresses! And then, how marvellous she looks
  When she puts one of them on! I dare say you've not seen –

PATAICOS: I have indeed.

POLEMON: For sheer splendour – they're worth
  a look.
  – Oh, there I go! What's splendour got to do with it?
  I'm raving mad, going on like that.

PATAICOS: No, not at all.

POLEMON: Do you think not? Anyhow, you must come and
  see. This way.

PATAICOS: Lead on, then. Let's go in.

    [*They go into Polemon's house.* MOSCHION *looks out
    of the door of Myrrhine's house, sees them disappearing,
    and emerges.*]

MOSCHION: Yes, go in and hang yourselves!
  To hell with you! 'Mine enemies with levelled spears
  Leapt forth upon me.' Scum! They haven't got the guts
  To storm a swallow's nest full of chicks.

    [SOSIAS *wanders out, still very drunk, and goes to sleep
    on the ground.*]

                And Daos said
  They'd got a squad of mercenaries – why, *that* must be

One of these famous mercenaries. – It's Sosias!
A one-man army!
                              – Of all the swarms of unhappy men
In the world today – and certainly, for whatever cause,
There's a fine crop of misery at this very moment
All over Hellas – I don't believe there's a single one
Of them all that has such wretched luck as I've been having.
When I got in, I did none of the things I usually do;
I didn't go to see my mother; I didn't call
For any of the servants; just went off to my own room
And lay down on my bed. I was perfectly composed.
I sent Daos to tell my mother I'd arrived –
Just that, no more. But Daos gave not a thought to me.
He found the table set for lunch, and sat straight down
And tucked in. Meanwhile I lay there, telling myself,
'Your mother'll be here any moment with a message
From your sweetheart suggesting how things might be
    arranged.'
And I was practising a little speech . . .

At this point about a hundred and fifty lines are missing. It is clear
that in the course of them Myrrhine's husband comes home. What
part he plays in the dénouement, whether he raises the 'flaming row'
Daos expected, we don't know. It can also be gathered that this
passage was largely occupied with Moschion's eavesdropping; first,
while indoors he has overheard a talk between Myrrhine and Glycera;
then he seems to have heard Pataicos soliloquizing after he came out
of Polemon's house; then when Glycera comes out he listens to her
conversation with Pataicos. What he picked up from these various
sources can be pieced together during the progress of the following
scene between Glycera and Pataicos. Glycera is trying to prove to
Pataicos that she is not involved with Moschion; if she had been,
she says, she would have acted differently.

GLYCERA: . . . . Think now, Pataicos: suppose I had taken
    refuge here,

Not to be Moschion's wife, mark you – for since I have
No money or family that's impossible – but to be
His mistress; could I ever have won his father and mother
To accept me? No, of course not. I'd have done my best
To keep it secret, and so would he. But instead of that
He went straight up and introduced me to his father.
When I came to this house I chose deliberately
A foolish course, one that would weigh against me, and
Perhaps invite you to suspect the worst of me.

PATAICOS: Wipe that suspicion out, and your good name is
   clear.

GLYCERA: Pataicos, did you think the same as all the others?
Did you come here assuming I was that sort of girl?

PATAICOS: No, no, as I worship Zeus! I do hope you can show
That the accusations are in fact unjust. Myself,
I believe they are. Yet, even so – go back to him!

GLYCERA: Polemon can find other girls to insult and bully.

PATAICOS: It was a wrong, but not a deliberate insult.

GLYCERA: No?
It was unspeakable, what he did to me. Look there!
    [*showing her hair*]
Could any slave-girl be a more revolting sight?

A gap here of sixteen lines, in which Glycera assures Pataicos that
she can prove she is free-born. She is telling him of the tokens she
possesses; Moschion is hidden and listening.

GLYCERA: . . . The old woman who brought me up gave me
   those things
As a gift from my own father and mother, telling me
Always to keep them with me and look after them.

PATAICOS: What do you want me to do?

GLYCERA: Have these things fetched for me.

PATAICOS: Do you mean that you have given up Polemon
   finally?
My dear girl, what are you planning?

GLYCERA: Just do this for me.
Will you?

PATAICOS: But this is silly. Above everything else
You ought to yield a little.

GLYCERA: I know what's best for me.

PATAICOS: You really mean that? Well; which of the servants knows
Where these things are?

GLYCERA: Doris knows. – Someone call her out.

PATAICOS: Yet all the same, Glycera, I beg you in God's name,
Make up your quarrel with Polemon on the kind of terms
I spoke about just now.

[*Enter* DORIS.]

DORIS: Here I am, madam. Anything I can do for you?

MOSCHION [*aside*]: Now I'll soon know the worst.

GLYCERA: Yes, Doris. Go and fetch
My little chest, the one where those embroideries
Are kept. I gave it to you to keep carefully;
I'm sure you know the one I mean. Go, hurry now.

[DORIS *goes*.]

MOSCHION [*aside*]: Great gods in glory! This is a most extra-
ordinary
Experience for me. Glycera, apparently,
Has not the slightest . . .

A gap of seven lines, in which Doris brings out the chest and
Pataicos begins looking at the contents.

PATAICOS: . . . This is just like that same embroidered scarf I
saw
Then – all those years ago! Look, this now, next to it –
Isn't this a goat, or cow, or some such animal?

GLYCERA: Why, dear Pataicos, that's no goat! Look, it's a
stag.

PATAICOS: Well, all I know is, it's got horns.

GLYCERA: What's this third thing?

PATAICOS: A winged horse – yes! These *are* my wife's things – my poor wife!

MOSCHION [*aside*]: Would you have thought it possible? I can't believe

That my own mother would do a thing so scandalous

As abandon her own child, the girl she'd borne herself.

If this *can* be believed, and Glycera is my sister,

To lose so sweet a sweetheart's just my rotten luck.

PATAICOS [*to himself*]: I had *two* children. Where's my son? More sadness yet.

GLYCERA: What is it? There's some question on your mind. Ask me.

PATAICOS: Where did you get these things?

GLYCERA: Why, I was wearing them

When I was picked up as a baby.

PATAICOS: Glycera,

Stand back a little – there; I want to see your face.

MOSCHION [*aside*]: This moment is the turning-point of my whole life.

PATAICOS: And when they found you, were you alone? I want to know.

GLYCERA: No indeed; my brother and I had been exposed together.

MOSCHION [*aside*]: That answers one of my questions.

PATAICOS: Then how did you come To be separated?

GLYCERA: I could tell you the whole story;

But – ask what I have a right to tell you – about myself.

The rest I must not speak of; I gave her my oath.

MOSCHION [*aside*]: There! that's a second point – it tallies perfectly.

She gave her oath to my mother. Oh, my head's going round!

PATAICOS: I see. Who was it found you, then? Who brought
    you up?

GLYCERA: A woman who found me lying there took care
    of me.

PATAICOS: Did she describe the sort of place she found you
    in?

GLYCERA: It was beside a spring, she said, shaded by trees.

PATAICOS: The man who took my children spoke of such a
    place.

GLYCERA: But who was he? – if it is proper for me to ask.

PATAICOS: A slave; but it was I who shirked caring for you.

GLYCERA: We were your true-born children, and you exposed
    us? Why?

PATAICOS: Many things unbelievable are done, my girl.
   Your mother died soon after giving birth to you;
   Also, one day before she died, one day before –

GLYCERA: What happened, father? Something dreadful!

PATAICOS: I became
   Penniless, after living in comfort all my life.

GLYCERA: Could all that happen in one day? How terrible!

PATAICOS: Yes; news came that the ship which earned my
    livelihood
   Was swallowed in the stormy surge of the Aegean.

GLYCERA: That was a cruel day for me.

PATAICOS: For a bankrupt man,
   To shoulder the extra burden of two mouths to feed
   Seemed to me then the sheerest folly.

GLYCERA:[1] . . .
   But were no tokens left with them for recognition?

PATAICOS: Yes, various necklaces were left with them, some
    clothes –
   Not many; and a little box.

GLYCERA: You're right so far;
   Now tell me what was in it.

1. The line is missing.

PATAICOS: Let me see – why, yes!
  There was a woman's girdle.
GLYCERA: Yes, there was! But, father,
  What figures were embroidered on it? Can you say?
PATAICOS: Yes; there were girls dancing together.
MOSCHION [*aside*]:   I begin
  To see it all.
GLYCERA: You're right; I have it still. What next?
PATAICOS: A golden headband. – Must I go through the
  whole list?
GLYCERA: Dear father, I'll stop doubting. Was I unfair?
  Forgive me!
        [*They embrace each other.*]

Here follows a gap of a hundred lines. It seems that the tokens which
Pataicos has just described are those which Moschion has in his
possession; and that at this point Moschion comes out of hiding and
is united with his father and sister. During the next few scenes
Glycera moves into Pataicos' house, and Polemon learns that she
and Moschion have been recognized as Pataicos' children. This makes
Polemon quite sure that Glycera will never again have anything to
do with him. He is talking with Doris.

POLEMON: . . . I meant to hang myself.
DORIS: No, no! Don't say that!
POLEMON: But what shall I do, Doris?
  How shall I live without her? Life's not worth living.
DORIS: Glycera says now, she'll go back to you –!
POLEMON: She says –
  Good gods!
DORIS: – if you're resolved from now on to have done
  With bad behaviour.
POLEMON: Doris, I give my oath to that.
  I will be faultless. Oh, your news is wonderful!
  Go to her now. Tomorrow, Doris, I'll set you free.
  Now this is what you are to say – listen! – She's gone!

Oh, raging, jealous Love!
You took my heart by storm. It was her brother, then,
And not her lover, that she kissed. I should have asked
For an explanation; instead, curse-ridden with jealousy,
I acted all in a moment like a drunken fool.
That's why I meant to hang myself; – and serve me right.
> [DORIS *reappears*.]
Doris, dear Doris, what's your news?

DORIS: Good news: she'll come!

POLEMON: She said that? She was making fun of me.

DORIS: Oh, no,
She was not, by Aphrodite! She was putting on
Her best gown; and her father stood and looked at her.
You ought to have offered sacrifice to thank the gods
For what they've done for her. This is her day of days,
And a gloomy face like yours is sheer impiety.

POLEMON: By Zeus, you're right. – The very thing – the
cook's indoors.
He must kill the sow, and we'll have a feast.

DORIS: But what about
The basket, and all the other things?

POLEMON: Basket? Don't worry!
We'll do all that stuff later. Tell the cook to kill
That sow. And better still, I'm going to take a wreath
From the altar here and wear it.

DORIS: That's a good idea;
You'll look much more persuasive.

POLEMON: Go and fetch Glycera,
Quickly!

DORIS: She was just coming, and her father, too.

POLEMON: Her father, too? Then what's in store for me?
> [*He hears the door of Pataicos' house opening, and runs
> into his own house.*]

DORIS [*laughing*]: Polemon!
Are you running away? What do you expect to see

When a door opens? A man-eating dragon? Well!
I'll go in too, and be of any use I can!

> [DORIS *follows Polemon into his house. Enter* PATAICOS
> *and* GLYCERA.]

PATAICOS [*to Glycera*]: I'm more than glad to hear you say
    you'll make it up.
When you've enjoyed good fortune, to be ready then
To accept honest amends – that proves you a true Greek.
– Here, boy! Run and call Polemon, quick!

POLEMON [*appearing at his door*]:   I'm coming.
I went in to arrange about a sacrifice
To thank the gods for this great news. I've just been told
Glycera's found her father – all her dreams come true.

PATAICOS: Yes; and I've something more to add: I here give
    you
Glycera, your wedded wife, to bear you lawful sons.

POLEMON: I take her.

PATAICOS: And a dowry of three talents.

POLEMON: Why,
That's marvellous!

PATAICOS: And, my boy, in future just forget
You're a soldier, and be less ferocious to your friends.

POLEMON: Good gods! Do you think, when I've just been
    within an inch
Of destroying my whole life, I'm going to turn ferocious
Ever again, or even dream of it? – Glycera,
Dearest! Only say you forgive me.

GLYCERA: Your crazy act
Has been our beginning of happiness.

POLEMON: Darling, it has.

GLYCERA: And that, of course, is why I forgive you!

POLEMON: Pataicos,
There's a banquet on; come and join us.

PATAICOS: Wait a moment, though.
One wedding's not enough. I've got to find a wife

For my son Moschion. [*He pulls Moschion forward.*]
   Who shall I get for Moschion?
   Why, there's Philinos' daughter –
MOSCHION: Oh, almighty gods
   Preserve me! ...

THE SAMIAN WOMAN

CHARACTERS

DEMEAS, *an Athenian citizen*
PARMENON, *house-slave of Demeas*
CHRYSIS, *a free-born woman from Samos, Demeas' mistress*
NICERATOS, *Demeas' neighbour, father of Plangon*
MOSCHION, *adopted son of Demeas*
A COOK
CHORUS *of wedding-guests*
An old Nurse; a number of slaves, male and female

*

Scene: A street in Athens, with Demeas' house on one side, Niceratos' house on the other.

The surviving text[1] begins with the opening of an Act; whether this is the second or the third Act is uncertain. The contents of the lost beginning of the play can be conjectured as follows:

Demeas is a prosperous bachelor. He has an adopted son called Moschion, whom he trusts and loves. A Samian woman called Chrysis lives with Demeas as his wife; because her parentage is unknown (and in any case is thought to be Samian, not Athenian) it is impossible under Athenian law for Demeas to make her his wife.

Moschion has fallen in love with Plangon, the daughter of his next-door neighbour Niceratos; but since Niceratos is too poor to provide Plangon with a dowry, the two have kept their love secret.

Demeas has been away from home for some months. During this time Chrysis has given birth to a child by him; and the child has died. At about the same time Plangon, unknown to her parents, has had a child by Moschion; and Chrysis has taken over this child and is rearing it.

Before going away, Demeas had apparently told Chrysis that if she bore a child during his absence it was to be exposed. (The reason why he did not want to have a child of his own is a mystery.) When Demeas returns, Chrysis tells him that her own (and his) child had died, but that this is a foundling which she is very anxious to keep. With difficulty she wins his consent that she shall rear the child.

Demeas decides it is time that Moschion was married, and tells him he is to marry Plangon. Moschion's eager acceptance of this plan causes Demeas some disquiet. The wedding is arranged, and preparations for a banquet are already in progress when the manuscript begins.

The surviving portions of the play fall clearly into three parts, which we shall call Scenes 1, 2 and 3.

1. It is tantalizing to learn that a papyrus containing a further considerable portion of this play is known to exist in a private collection, not yet made available to scholars or to the public. See A. Dain, *La Survie de Ménandre*, in *Maia* 15 (1963), pp. 278ff.

SCENE ONE

DEMEAS: I tell you this: a man who goes abroad and leaves
His mistress alone at home is either mad or else
He very soon will be. Just when he's made a nice profit,
He's sunk again with a dead loss. I'd just gone in
To hurry on preparations for my son's wedding.
I was telling them all, 'Moschion's to be married today;
So just get everything ready, clean the whole place up,
Make cakes, and fill the basket for the ceremony.'
Well, things were going smoothly enough; though naturally
The sudden hurry put them all in a bit of a stew; –
And there, lying on a bed, just shoved down out of the
    way,
Was the baby, howling. The maids were shouting, 'Where's
    the flour?
Fetch in some water; hand me the oil; put on more coal!'
Well, I was issuing stores, and helping; and I'd just
Gone into the store-room, where I was busy choosing out
Still more stuff, keeping an eye on everything; and so
I didn't come out at once; and while I was still in there
A woman came down the stairs into the room that's just
Opposite the store-room door. It's a sort of weaving-room;
The way upstairs is through it; and I go through it too
To get to the store-room. Now, this woman was once nurse
To Moschion; she's free now, but I keep her on
As a servant; she's quite elderly. Well, she saw the baby
Left there alone and crying. She had no idea
I was in the store-room; for all she knew, she was safe in
    saying
Whatever she pleased. She went up to the kid, and began
The usual baby-talk – 'Duckie, sweetie-pie,' says she,

And 'Aren't you a beautiful boy?' and 'Where's your
  mummy gone?'
She kissed it, carried it up and down; and when it stopped
Crying, 'Oh, dear,' says she, 'it seems only yesterday
I was nursing Moschion, a darling little mite like this.
Now Moschion's got a son of his own; and someone else
Will nurse it, and in turn . . .¹
Some little maid came running in, and the old woman
Called to her, 'Give the baby his bath, lazybones!
This is a fine way to go on,' says she, 'to leave
The baby uncared-for on his father's wedding-day!'
Then straight away the little maid said, 'Hush, you fool –
Talking like that! Master's in the house.' – 'No! Is he?
  Where?'
– 'He's in the store-room.' Then she changed her voice a
  bit;
'Nurse, the mistress is calling you; go on, be quick.
– He hasn't heard a thing; that's a bit of luck.' So then
The old woman went off, muttering, 'Dear, oh dear,
My tongue again!' – and disappeared. Then I stepped
  out,
Quite quiet and calm – the way I came out here just now,
Exactly as if I'd seen nothing, heard nothing; – and there
I saw Chrysis herself in 'he courtyard holding the child,
And as I went past she was putting it to her breast.
So this at least is certain, that the baby's hers;
But who's the father? Me? Or . . .? Friends, I'd rather not
Say anything, or even guess; but I put to you
The plain facts, and the words I heard with my own ears.
No, I'm not angry – yet. And as for the young man,
His behaviour up to now has been exemplary,
I'll take my oath on that; and his attitude to me
Could not have been more proper or more honourable.
But then again, when I realize that this woman

1. There is a gap here of five and a half lines.

Who said those words, was Moschion's nurse, and never
  dreamt
She was speaking in my hearing; and when I reflect
That it was Chrysis who so doted on the child,
And – against my will – insisted we should bring it up,
I fly right off the handle. – Oh, here's Parmenon
Back from the market; just at the right moment too.
I'll wait a little, while he takes that Cook indoors.

[DEMEAS *stands aside. Enter* PARMENON *and* COOK.]

PARMENON: Here, Cook, for the gods' sake hurry, now! I
  can't think why
  You carry that chopper round with you; your tongue's
  enough
  To make mincemeat of anything. Can't you keep quiet?

COOK: You're a poor ignorant fool.

PARMENON: What, me?

COOK: I reckon so.
  Why grumble at me, simply because I want to know
  How many tables you intend to serve, how many
  Ladies are coming, what time you want dinner ready,
  Whether I'll need to get a butler, whether you've got
  Crockery enough of your own, whether your bakery's
  Indoors or out, whether you're adequately equipped
  With all the other –

PARMENON: Look here, mate, you're driving me
  Right round the bend; I tell you straight, you give me fits.
  You beat all, you do.

COOK: Boil your head.

PARMENON: And the same to you,
  And many of 'em. Go on in now.

        [*The* COOK *with his assistants enters the house.*
        PARMENON *is about to follow him, when* DEMEAS
        speaks.]

DEMEAS: Parmenon!

PARMENON [*turning*]: Someone called me?

DEMEAS: Yes, I did.

PARMENON: Oh – good morning, sir.

DEMEAS [*sternly*]: Just put that hamper indoors; then come
   back here.

PARMENON [*alarmed*]:   Yes, sir –
   God bless you, sir – and me too.
       [*He goes indoors.*]

DEMEAS [*to himself*]:   I'm sure Parmenon
   Doesn't miss much; whatever's going on – he knows.
   He's a busybody, if ever there was one. – Here he comes.
       [PARMENON, *appearing in the doorway, calls back to*
       Chrysis inside.]

PARMENON: Chrysis, see that the Cook gets everything he
   wants;
   And, for the gods' sake, keep that old crone's fingers out
   Of the pie-dishes. – Here I am, sir; what do you wish me
   to do?

DEMEAS: Wish you to do? Come here – away from the door.
   – Further.

PARMENON: Yes, sir.

DEMEAS: Now listen, Parmenon. I swear to you
   By the gods, I've not the slightest wish – for many reasons –
   To give you a flogging.

PARMENON: A flogging, sir? Why, what have I
   done?

DEMEAS: You're hiding something from me, I've discovered.

PARMENON: No, sir!
   By Dionysos, by Apollo and Saviour Zeus,
   By Asclepios –

DEMEAS: Stop, now, none of that!

PARMENON: You're guessing wrong,
   You are, sir, strike me dead, sir!

DEMEAS: Look me in the eyes.

PARMENON: I'm looking.

DEMEAS: Tell me: whose child is it?

PARMENON [*playing for time*]: I'm looking, sir.

DEMEAS: I asked you, Whose child is it?

PARMENON: Why, it's Chrysis' child.

DEMEAS: And who is the father?

PARMENON: You, of course.

DEMEAS: That's done for you.
I'm well aware of the whole business: that this child
Is Moschion's; that you know it is; and that Chrysis
Is rearing him for Moschion.

PARMENON: Who told you this?

DEMEAS: I know it. Still, just answer me: whose is this child?

PARMENON: I've told you, sir. – But nobody need know –

DEMEAS: Nobody
Need know? [*To a slave*] You there, hand me a whip for
   this damned liar.

PARMENON: No, don't, sir, don't for God's sake.

DEMEAS [*taking whip from slave*]: I'll tattoo your hide.

PARMENON: Tattoo my –

DEMEAS: Yes, I'll do it now.

PARMENON [*breaking free and running for it*]: Help, help!

DEMEAS: Here, you!
Come here, you devil! Hold him, there! Oh, oh, oh, oh! –
O all you host of heaven! O earth! What else?
And shall I couple hell? – Come off it, Demeas!
Why shout like a fool? Steady now – take a grip of yourself.
Moschion hasn't wronged you! [*To audience*] To say that,
   my friends,
May seem surprising; but it's true. Supposing, now,
He had done this thing deliberately, or in the throes
Of passionate love, or simply because he hated me,
His behaviour to me now would be what it was then –
Hostile. Instead, he has cleared himself by welcoming
This marriage I've provided. Yes: what drove him on
Was not love, as I at first imagined, but the wish
To escape at all costs from that Helen of mine indoors!

Yes, she is the one responsible. It's obvious:
She found him drunk, perhaps, or not himself. Strong wine
And young blood, even when a boy's quite innocent
Of wrong intentions, lead him on to anything.
I find it in every way incredible, that one
Who's well-behaved and decent to all and sundry, should
Behave like this – to *me*! If he were twenty times
An adopted son, not mine by birth, I'd still judge him
By his known character, not by his origin.

But she – the dirty slut! The whore, the – why go on?
It'll do no good; so be a man, Demeas; forget
What you would like to remember. Stop longing for her.
What's happened is bad luck; well, then, for the boy's sake
Hide it as best you can – but throw that Samian bitch
Out on her ear! To hell with her! You've got an excuse –
She kept the child; so, best not say another word.
Keep a stiff lip; have pride enough to take the blow.

[*The* COOK *appears at Demeas' door.*]

COOK: He must be out here somewhere. [*Bawling*] Hi, there!
    Parmenon!
Run out on me, he has; done not a stroke of work!

    [DEMEAS, *suddenly reminded of the wedding, turns to go
    indoors.*]

DEMEAS: You get to hell out of my way!

    [*Exit* DEMEAS.]

COOK [*staggering*]:   Whew! Heracles!
What's going on? – Parmenon! – Some aged lunatic
Has just pelted indoors! What's happening? – Parmenon! –
I'll take my oath he's raving mad. – Oh, help! I've left
My dishes lying all over the place – he'll smash them all
To bits! – No, here he comes again. – Oh, Parmenon,
I hope you roast in hell for hiring me on this job!
– I'll stand here out of his way.

    [CHRYSIS *runs out of the house,* DEMEAS *following.*]

DEMEAS: Well, didn't you hear me? Go!

CHRYSIS: Go where, for pity's sake?

DEMEAS: To hell, and lose no time.

CHRYSIS: Oh, cruel! [*She bursts into tears.*]

DEMEAS: Yes, cruel – that's it: a flood of tears to make
Me sorry for you. But I'll stop your goings-on –

CHRYSIS: What goings-on?

DEMEAS: Nothing. You've got your baby now;
You've got the nurse. All right – clear out.

CHRYSIS: Is this because
I kept the baby?

DEMEAS: Because of that, yes; and –

CHRYSIS: And what?

DEMEAS: Just that. That started everything.

CHRYSIS: I don't understand.

DEMEAS: You had no notion how to live in style.

CHRYSIS: In style?
What *are* you talking about?

DEMEAS: When you first came to me,
Remember, you wore a cotton dress, a cheap one too.

CHRYSIS: Well, what of that?

DEMEAS: Then I was everything to you,
When you were poor.

CHRYSIS: Well, who is now?

DEMEAS: Don't talk to me.
You've got all your own things. I'm giving you as well
Your maids, and all your jewellery. Now leave my house.

CHRYSIS [*aside*]: This is a fit of anger. I must plead with him.
[*To Demeas*] Now look, my dear –

DEMEAS: Are you arguing?

CHRYSIS: Don't snap at me.

DEMEAS: From now on, Chrysis, some one else'll enjoy my home,
And think herself lucky.

CHRYSIS: What do you mean?

DEMEAS: You've borne a son;
That was all you wanted.

CHRYSIS [*aside*]: He's not snapping at me yet.
[*To Demeas*] All the same –

DEMEAS: If you argue with me, you
wretch, I'll break your head.

CHRYSIS [*aside*]: My own fault. [*To Demeas*] See, I'm going
now.

DEMEAS: Thank heaven for that.
Up in the city, you'll soon find out your natural bent.
Your type, my girl, can only earn ten drachmas a time;
They trot round all the dinner-parties and drink themselves
To death with neat wine; or if they can't manage that,
They live and starve. You'll be as good as any of them,
I'll bet, at learning how it's done. And then you'll know
Just what you did when you behaved like that to me.
[*As Chrysis moves towards him*] Stay where you are!
[DEMEAS *goes into his house*.]

CHRYSIS: What shall I do? What shall I do?
[*Enter* NICERATOS *with a slave bringing a live sheep*.]

NICERATOS: This sheep I've got, when sacrificed, will satisfy
All due requirements for the gods and goddesses.
It's got some blood; sufficient gall; some lovely bones;
Large spleen; – all things essential to Olympians.
When those are offered, I'll cut up and give away
As tit-bits to my friends all I'll have left – the skin!
[*The slave takes the sheep into the house*.]
Why, Heracles! What's going on? That can't be Chrysis
Standing out on the doorstep weeping? Yes, it is! –
What on earth's happened?

CHRYSIS: What do you think? Your worthy friend
Has turned me out.

NICERATOS: Good heavens above! Who? Demeas?

CHRYSIS: Yes, Demeas.

NICERATOS: What for?

CHRYSIS: Because of the child.

NICERATOS: Why, yes;
My women-folk were telling me you'd taken on
A child, and meant to bring it up. A mad idea –
Still, Demeas is soft-hearted.

CHRYSIS: He wasn't angry at all
At first, but only later on; in fact, just now
He told me himself to get ready everything indoors
For the wedding today; while I'm in the middle of it
He bursts in, charges at me like a lunatic;
And now he's locked me out.

NICERATOS: Can Demeas be mad?

At this point the MS breaks off. It is clear that during the rest of this scene Niceratos takes pity on Chrysis and invites her to stay in his house for the present; and she goes in with him, accompanied by the old Nurse carrying the child. In several subsequent scenes, now lost, it would appear that Moschion learns about the suspicions Demeas has harboured, and clears himself to his father's satisfaction; explaining that the mother of the child is Plangon, and admitting that he, Moschion, is the father. Demeas meanwhile continues to prepare for the wedding, and is anxious to receive Chrysis back into his house. The MS resumes in the middle of a dialogue between Demeas and Niceratos, in which Demeas has evidently told Niceratos that the baby is Plangon's, but not that its father is Moschion.

SCENE TWO

DEMEAS, NICERATOS.

DEMEAS: ... My dear man, don't get too worried over a
   little slip like that.
   You go back indoors and –
NICERATOS: Little? Do you call that a little slip?
   It's the end, I tell you; upsets everything; it's all finished!
       [NICERATOS *rushes despairing into his house.*]
DEMEAS: Yes, by Zeus! If once he learns the truth, he'll burst
   and roar with rage.
   He's a rough type, a real swine, stubborn as a mule. – Yet,
   look at me:
   I'm a swine too! Why should I suspect my son of such a
   crime?
   I, of all men! Damn it, I don't deserve to live.
       [*An uproar is heard from Niceratos' house.*]
                                              Now what in hell
   Can that row be?
       [*He goes to the door to listen.*]
                   Yes, it is! He's bellowing, 'Make up the fire!'
   Says he'll kill the baby and burn it. That's the next thing we
   shall see –
   Roasting grandson! – Gods! he's coming. What a man!
   He's much more like
   A tornado or a thunderbolt.
       [*Enter* NICERATOS.]
NICERATOS: Demeas, it's scandalous!
   Chrysis there – she's plotting against me.
DEMEAS: What?
NICERATOS: Yes! She's induced my wife
   And the girl to back her up in not confessing a single
   thing;

Holds on to the brat by main force, swears she'll never let
   it go.

Don't let it surprise you if I kill that woman.

DEMEAS: Kill Chrysis?

NICERATOS: She knows all about the whole thing!

DEMEAS: You'll do nothing of the sort!

NICERATOS: I just thought I'd give you warning, that's all.
        [He rushes back into his house.]

DEMEAS: The man's raving mad.

He's whipped in again. Everything's going wrong. What
   is a man to do?

All I know is, never before was I in such an unholy mess.

Should I now tell him the whole truth? That would, after
   all, be best –

Help, Apollo! Someone's coming out again!

        [From Niceratos' house CHRYSIS *enters holding the baby*
        and pursued by NICERATOS.]

CHRYSIS: What shall I do?

Where can I go? He's going to take my baby!

DEMEAS [*pointing to his own door*]:   Chrysis, come this way!

CHRYSIS [*who does not at first see Demeas*]: Who's that?

DEMEAS: Run inside here.

NICERATOS: Here, you! Where are you off to?

DEMEAS [*to audience*]:   Watch me now –

Heavyweight champion! [*To Niceratos*] What's this? Who
   are you chasing round?

NICERATOS: Now, Demeas,

You keep out of this. I mean to get that baby. Then I'll
   hear

What these women have got to say about the business.

DEMEAS [*to audience, indicating Niceratos*]:   Mental case.

– Oh, you'll hit me, will you?

NICERATOS [*hitting him*]:   Yes, I will.

DEMEAS [*to Chrysis*]:   You get indoors, damn it!

– All right, here's for you, then.

[*He hits Niceratos. To Chrysis*]

                Run in; he's a stronger man than me.

    [*Exit* CHRYSIS.]

NICERATOS: There now – you laid hands on me first. I'll
    swear that in court.

DEMEAS: And you
    Take a stick to a free-born woman and chase her, do you?

NICERATOS: Blackmailer!

DEMEAS: So are you, then.

NICERATOS: You won't let me have that child?

DEMEAS: Don't make me laugh!
    When it's mine?

NICERATOS: It isn't yours.

    [*He pushes Demeas aside and goes towards Demeas'
    door.*]

DEMEAS: Help friends! I'm being attacked!

NICERATOS: Go on,
    Bawl your head off! I'm going in to kill that woman.

DEMEAS: What shall I do?
    This is frightful. I won't let him. – Where are you going?
    You stay here!

NICERATOS: Don't you lay a finger on me.

DEMEAS: Just control yourself.

NICERATOS: Look here,
    Demeas, you're pulling a fast one on me – why, it's obvious:
    You know all about this business.

DEMEAS: Listen while I tell you, then;
    And – you keep your hands off Chrysis.

NICERATOS: Your son Moschion – hasn't he
    Simply fooled me over Plangon?

DEMEAS: Rubbish! First, he'll marry her.
    Next, things aren't as you imagine. Come now, let's walk
    up and down
    Here and talk it over.

NICERATOS: Walk up and . . . ?

DEMEAS: Why not? Take yourself in hand.

[*They walk up and down together.*]

Tell me now, Niceratos: you've often heard, in tragic plays,

Stories of how Zeus once turned himself to gold, and trickled down

Through the roof, and went to bed with a young girl imprisoned there?

NICERATOS: What of it?

DEMEAS: Just this: one's got to be prepared for anything!
Has your roof, I wonder, got a leak or two?

NICERATOS: My whole roof leaks!
What's that got to do with it?

DEMEAS: Why, Zeus sometimes comes down as rain,
Sometimes gold. Well, don't you see? It's Zeus's doing! Question solved

In a moment.[1]

NICERATOS: What's all this? Is it bran-mash you're feeding me?

DEMEAS: No, by Apollo I'm not. In fact, you aren't one little bit worse off

Than Danae's father. Look: if Zeus was pleased to lie with Danae,

Why should not your daughter –

NICERATOS: But this is outrageous. Moschion's
Made a stuffed owl of me.

DEMEAS: Moschion will marry her, never fear.
This is a miracle-child, you take my word for it. Why, I could name [*his eye wanders over the audience*]

Thousands walking round in Athens – born from gods! And do you cry

Stinking fish because your daughter's had a little accident?

---

1. Perhaps Demeas means: Your leaky roof lets in rain-water; but when it let Zeus, i.e., Moschion, in, it allied you, a poor man, with me, your rich neighbour, and was thus a shower of gold like Danae's – a tactful and humorous way of pointing out one advantage that will come of the marriage.

[*He points to a member of the audience.*]

Look, to begin with – there! The universal sponger, Chaerephon!

Wouldn't you say *he*'s immortal?

NICERATOS: Probably. What do *I* care?

I'm not going to argue over nothing.

DEMEAS: Well, you're very wise.

Look at Androcles, now, living all these years! Trotting about;

Lots of boy friends; walks along with grey hair dyed a lovely black;

He won't die, even if you cut his throat. Then isn't he a god?

Come, now, make your offerings; pray that all will turn out happily.

You and I will be 'in-laws' now – and a very good thing too.

As for my son, he'll get married – and he'd better!

NICERATOS: Yes, you're right.

But [*bridling up again*] if I'd just caught him when he –

DEMEAS: Tut, tut! Don't get blood-pressure!

Are things ready in your house yet?

NICERATOS [*with rueful sarcasm*]:   Yes, oh yes – Belshazzar's feast!

DEMEAS: You're a wit!

          [*Exit* NICERATOS *into his house.*]

[*To himself*] Well! All those miserable suspicions I endured!

Thank the gods I've found there's no truth in them – thank the blessed gods!

          [*Exit* DEMEAS *into his house. A* CHORUS *of wedding-guests enters and gives a performance of music and dancing.*]

SCENE THREE

Enter MOSCHION *from Demeas' house.*

MOSCHION: A little while ago I was extremely pleased
　　To have cleared myself – with difficulty – on all counts;
　　I reckoned that was quite a piece of well-earned luck.
　　But now I'm somewhat more in my right mind, and set
　　One thing against another, I feel furious –
　　Yes, absolutely livid, to think what my father
　　Suspected me of doing. Hell! If Plangon now
　　Were in a happier situation, and if I
　　Weren't hampered by so much that makes a slave of me –
　　By vows, affection, long acquaintance, and desire –
　　I'd not give the old man a second chance to make
　　Such accusations to my face; I'd get to hell
　　Out of this city, away to Bactria, Caria –
　　Somewhere out East, and do a spell of soldiering.
　　As it is – for your sake, Plangon darling, I'll refrain
　　From heroism; in fact, it's quite unthinkable –
　　Forbidden by the new master of my purpose, Love.
　　Still, I don't feel like overlooking the whole affair
　　And showing myself submissive and degenerate.
　　If nothing else, I'll drop a word about taking off,
　　And give the old man a fright; so that another time
　　He'll take care not to ignore my sensibilities
　　When once he sees that I don't laugh off this incident.
　　　　　　[*He sees Parmenon approaching.*]
　　Why, here's the very man I want, and just in time.
　　　　　[MOSCHION *stands aside as* PARMENON *soliloquizes.*]
PARMENON: By Zeus Almighty, what an utter fool I've been!
　　A contemptible fool. I just took fright and ran away
　　From my master, though I'd done nothing wrong. What
　　　　had I done,

To run away? Let's look at everything, point by point.
First, my young master went to bed with a free-born girl.
No blame for that, surely, on Parmenon. The girl
Got pregnant – that's not Parmenon's fault. The baby then
Came to our house – young master brought it, I didn't.
One of the slaves indoors told Master about it – well,
Has Parmenon done anything wrong there? Nothing.
Then why on earth do you run away, you blundering fool?
He frightened me. – Ridiculous! – He threatened he'd
Mark me for life. – What reason could he have had for that?
– It makes not a jot of difference, when you're marked for life,
Whether you've deserved it or not deserved it. In either case
It's just not nice.

MOSCHION: Hey, there!

PARMENON: Good day, Sir.

MOSCHION: Cut that talk
And get indoors, quick.

PARMENON: Yes, and do what, Sir?

MOSCHION: Bring me out
A cloak and sword.

PARMENON: A sword? For *you*, Sir?

MOSCHION: Yes, and quick.

PARMENON: What for?

MOSCHION: Get going; do as I tell you; and say nothing.

PARMENON: But what's it all about?

MOSCHION: If I get hold of a strap –

PARMENON: No, no! I'm going.

MOSCHION: Go, then.

[*Exit* PARMENON.]

Now my father'll come.
He'll beg me to stay on here; and he'll beg in vain –
For a while; he must. Then, when I judge the moment's come,

191

I'll yield to him. If I can only act it plausibly! –
And that, Dionysos knows, is not my strongest point.
Well, this is it; he's coming.

[*Enter* PARMENON.]

PARMENON: Sir, you're out of date entirely with what's
    going on indoors!
You know nothing, you've heard nothing; so you've got
    into a state
All for nothing. Drop all this and join the party.

MOSCHION: Haven't you brought –

PARMENON: They're all busy with your wedding – filling
    high the sparkling bowl –
Flame of incense leaps to heaven –

MOSCHION: You rat, where's my cloak and sword?

PARMENON: Oh, forget it! All your friends are waiting for
    you this half-hour.
Go and fetch your bride; lose no more time, this is your
    lucky day!
You've got nothing to look glum at. Cheer up! Well,
    what more d'you want?

MOSCHION: Are you lecturing me, you horse-thief? [*He hits
    him.*]

PARMENON: What's that for, Sir?

MOSCHION: You run in
Quick and bring me what I told you.

PARMENON: Look, my lip's cut open, Sir.

MOSCHION: You still talking?

PARMENON: No, I'm going. Look at the reward I get!

MOSCHION: Still here?

PARMENON [*opening the door*]: See for yourself now – there's
    your wedding in full swing!

MOSCHION [*suddenly changing his tone*]: Go in
Quickly – then come out and tell me –

        [PARMENON *goes in.*]

              Now my father's bound to come.

Wait – there's one point I'd forgotten: suppose, instead of
  begging me
To stay here, he flies into a rage and says, All right, then,
  go!
What'll I do then? He's not likely to say that; but anything's
Possible. I'd look ridiculous if I had to eat my words.

Here the manuscript ends; and the reader may conjecture the rest
of the play according to his fancy. Almost certainly Moschion's
surmise must prove true; and Demeas seems due for some degree of
moral awakening and repentance; while to Chrysis surely belongs
the final act of forgiveness. One fragment remains, probably from
the final scene of merrymaking:

Bring the incense; make the fire up, Tryphe ...

THE HERO

The outline[1] of the plot is as follows:

A young unmarried woman, Myrrhine, having given birth to twins, a boy and a girl, exposed them. They were found by a farm-bailiff, Tibeios, who took them to his home and brought them up. Later Myrrhine married the man who had seduced her, Laches. In course of time Tibeios died, owing money to Laches; to pay off the debt, the boy, Gorgias, went with his sister, Plangon, to work for Laches. Neither he nor Laches knew of their relationship. A slave of Laches, Daos, fell in love with Plangon, supposing her to be a fellow-slave. Plangon, however, had already been seduced by a neighbour, Pheidias. Daos wanted to take upon himself responsibility for Plangon's pregnancy; and the mother, Myrrhine, not knowing that Daos was innocent, was very angry. When everything became known, the old man Laches found his own children and recognized them by tokens left with them when they were exposed; and the seducer, Pheidias, willingly married Plangon.

The only surviving fragment of any size is a part of the Prologue, a conversation between Daos and another slave, Getas. There is some evidence to suggest that after this Prologue a god appeared to give an exposition of the plot, as in *The Unkindest Cut*; and that here the god was a 'Hero', the spirit of some famous ancestor who was worshipped as tutelary deity of the household of Laches and Myrrhine.

1. This outline is adapted from the metrical Argument prefixed to the text.

PROLOGUE

GETAS, DAOS.

GETAS: Daos, it seems to me you must have carried out
    Some frightful crime, and now you're sweating at the
      thought
    Of being chained to the treadmill. Something's wrong,
      that's clear.
    Why do you beat your head like that? and then stand still
    And tear your hair out? and then groan?
DAOS: Oh, gods above!
GETAS: I'm right, I knew it: you bad lot! Then wouldn't it
    Be wise to hand over to me, for a little while,
    Any small savings you may have, in case you bring
    More trouble on yourself? You won't? Then I'm fed up
    With you, and no wonder: always suspicious!
DAOS: What on earth,
    For God's sake, are you drooling about? I'm in a spot.
    It's got me down. I simply don't know what to do.
GETAS: Well, it's your own fault, damn you!
DAOS: Friend, for pity's sake,
    Don't damn a man when he's in love.
GETAS: What's that? In love?
DAOS: Yes, I'm in love.
GETAS: Your master gives you more than double
    The standard ration. A bad thing, Daos. It's probably
    Just overeating.
DAOS: It's not the stomach, it's the heart,
    Getas. She's a young, innocent girl who lives with us,
    A slave like me; and every time I look at her –
GETAS: A slave, is she?
DAOS: Well, in a way, yes. There was a man
    Tibeios, a shepherd, who lived here in Ptelea –

A slave, when he was young. He had two children,
  twins –
Or so he always said; one was this girl Plangon
That I'm in love with –

GETAS: Yes, I follow.

DAOS: – and a boy
Called Gorgias.

GETAS: That lad who works as a shepherd here?

DAOS: Yes. Well, Tibeios their father, getting on in years,
  To help him feed the children, borrowed money from
  My master Laches; and again, when times were hard
  And prices high, borrowed some more; and then he died.

GETAS: Because your master wouldn't give him a third loan?

DAOS: Perhaps. Well, when Tibeios was dead, young
  Gorgias
Borrowed a little more, and with it gave the old man
A proper funeral and a grave; and then came here
To us, bringing his sister with him; and here he stays
While he works off the debt.

GETAS: And what does Plangon do?

DAOS: She's with my mistress; helps at spinning; serves at
  meals.

GETAS [*mocking Daos' indignant tone*]: A young girl serves at
  table?

DAOS: You're making fun of me.
I tell you, she's –

GETAS: No, not at all!

DAOS: You'd never tell
She wasn't free-born; she's so modest, so –

GETAS: Well, now,
What are you doing to help your cause?

DAOS: I've tried nothing
Underhand. I told my master all about it; and he's
Promised to let her live with me, once he's discussed
The matter with her brother.

GETAS: Well, then, why are you
So gloomy?

DAOS: Because my master's been away three months
On some business in Lemnos. Oh! If only he'd
Come safely home!

GETAS: I long for that as much as you.
Heaven bring him back to us!

DAOS: Why don't we offer sacrifice?
The gods might send a blessing.

GETAS: A most suitable
And excellent plan. If I were in love, I'd sacrifice
Regardless, however poor I was – you bet I would.

        [*He turns to an imaginary person in the audience.*]

Hey! Firewood-merchant! Bring us a load of firewood,
    quick,
For a sacrifice!

DAOS: Getas, have you never been in love?

GETAS: No; I never had a full stomach.

A number of small fragments, of two lines or less, can be assigned
to later scenes in this play; but the only one that seems worth adding
here is this, from a speech of Daos to Myrrhine:

DAOS: Mistress, there's nothing in this world stronger than
    love.
Why, even Zeus, who is king of all the gods in heaven,
Cannot resist, but yields to love in everything.

The course of events in the rest of the play seems to be as follows:
    In the later part of the Prologue Daos tells Getas that the real
reason for his distress is his knowledge that Plangon is pregnant, and
near her time. He does not know who was responsible; but is
prepared to assume responsibility himself. During the course of the
action Plangon's child is born; and Laches returns from Lemnos.
Myrrhine finds in Plangon's possession some tokens which she
recognizes as those which she left with her own children when she

exposed them. She has never told her husband Laches that she had these children before she married him; and she is terrified at the thought that he may discover it. In some way, however, it is found that these same tokens also identify Laches as the father of the twins. Thus they are proved free-born, and are accepted by their parents. The father of Plangon's child is Pheidias, a rich neighbour, who loves her and wants to marry her; now that she is known to be free-born this becomes possible, and the wedding is arranged. Daos is probably consoled for his disappointment by being given his freedom.

THE FARMER

On the stage are two houses. In one of them lives a poor widow called Myrrhine, with her daughter, whose name we do not know. In the other lives a rich citizen, who has a son by his first wife and a daughter, Hedeia, by his second. This son has just returned home from Corinth. Before he went away he had an affair with the poor widow's daughter, and she is now pregnant. The son is in love with her and wants to marry her; but his father, not wishing his son to marry a girl with no dowry, has during the boy's absence decided that he shall marry his half-sister Hedeia; and hearing that the youth would return home today, has made all arrangements for an immediate wedding.

The widow has also a son called Gorgias; he is at present in the country, working under a farmer called Cleainetos. Gorgias is the son of Myrrhine's late husband; but Myrrhine's daughter is older, and is the child of another man – in fact, of Cleainetos, who had an affair with Myrrhine before her marriage. Cleainetos has a bad conscience about his desertion of Myrrhine; he has never married; and though reasonably well off, still lives a life of rigorous labour on the farm.

In the first surviving scene the rich citizen's son comes out of his father's house in great agitation and addresses the audience. He tells of his entanglement with his poor neighbour's daughter; of his love for her, and his fear that the present situation may cause enmity between himself and her half-brother Gorgias.

... But what I'd done was not a crime; I didn't feel
Guilty. Well, Gorgias then was spending all his time
Away in the country; and I went off on certain business
To Corinth. While I was there, the disaster happened
    which
Has simply shattered me. When I came home last night I
    found
Another wedding being prepared for me; the gods
All wreathed in flowers, my father offering sacrifice.

And who was the bride's father? My father was that
  too!
You see, I've a half-sister who's the daughter of
My father's present wife. So I'm in a cleft stick;
How I can struggle out of it I just don't know.
I only know I'm in a spot. I've just walked out
Of the house without saying anything. Suppose I quit
This wedding: I'm very fond of my half-sister, and
To abandon her like that would be unkind, unfair,
A breach of family loyalty. And then again
I thought I'd knock at Myrrhine's door, and talk it over
With the girl I really love; but still I hesitate.
Her brother Gorgias may be home now from the farm –
I just don't know. I've got to think of everything.
Well, for the moment I'll clear off, and try to plan
One thing: how to escape this wedding.

> [*Exit.* MYRRHINE *enters from her house, with an old
> slave or nurse called Philinna.*]

MYRRHINE: Listen, dear:
You're a friend I can trust. That's why I talk to you,
Philinna, and tell you all my troubles. So now you know
Just how things are.

PHILINNA: I do; and by the holy gods,
After what I've heard, my dear, I've a good mind to go
Straight to that door and call out the disgraceful scamp
And tell him what I think of him.

MYRRHINE: Philinna, please!
I'd rather let him go.

PHILINNA: What, that blackguard? Go where?
To hell, that's where he ought to go! When he's behaved
Like that to our poor girl, is he to marry now?

MYRRHINE: Now, do have done with all this talk. Look who
  comes here:
It's Daos from the farm. Let's stand aside a while.

PHILINNA: Why, what concern of ours is Daos?

MYRRHINE: All the same

It's quite a good idea.

It is not clear whose slave Daos is, the rich citizen's or Cleainetos'.

[DAOS *comes in accompanied by another slave called*
SYROS, *and carrying a sheaf of flowers and sprays.*]

DAOS: I don't know any man that works a better farm.
Got a real sense of duty, that land has! Look there:
Myrtle-berries; fine ivy-sprays; a heap of flowers ...[1]
And anything else you like to plant – it pays you back
Not more, nor less; just fair, good measure. – Here,
Syros,
Take everything we've brought, the whole lot, straight
indoors;
It's all for the wedding. – Why, good day to you,
Myrrhine.

MYRRHINE: Good day to you too.

DAOS [*To Philinna*]: Noble and distinguished Madam,
I didn't see you. How are you getting on? Listen:
I'm going to feast you with good news – or rather, with
News of good things to come, God willing; and I want
To be the first to tell you. A few days ago
Cleainetos, whose farm your son is working on,
Was digging in his vineyard, when he cut his leg
Wide open – a grand gash!

MYRRHINE: Oh, no! How terrible!

DAOS: Courage! there's more yet. Three days later, from
this wound
The old man had a swelling ulcer; fever then
Set in; and he was in a bad state.

PHILINNA: Is this what
You call good news? You rubbish, sweep yourself away!

MYRRHINE: Now keep quiet, Granny!

___
1. A line continuing the list is missing at this point.

DAOS: Then, just when he needs someone
To look after him, his house-slaves, like the barbarous lot
They are, all begin saying, This puts paid to him;
This is good-bye, they say. But your son Gorgias –
You'd think it was his own father, the way he tended him.
Rubbed him with oil, washed out the ulcer, brought him
    food,
And cheered him up – for a wound like that is dangerous.
In fact, his care has brought the old man back to life.

MYRRHINE: Oh, splendid lad!

DAOS: Yes – and, well done Cleainetos!
For, while he was recovering, lying quiet indoors,
Free from his spade and all his troubles – well, you know
The rough, hard life he lives – he questioned Gorgias
About himself and his affairs; no doubt he knew
Something already. So the lad got talking to him;
And when he put in a word about his sister and you,
And the trouble you've had here, the old man, deeply
    moved
In a way that's not uncommon, felt that on every score
He should make some return for services received.
So, being old and lonely, he made up his mind:
He's going to marry your daughter! Yes, he's given his
    word.
So that's the long and the short of it. He and Gorgias
Will be here any minute; and the old man will take
Your daughter back with him to the farm. So you'll be
    able
To stop your daily fight with that intractable
And sullen monster, Poverty; especially since
You live in the town here. Either one should have money,
Or live in a place where one's misfortunes aren't laid bare
For all the world to witness. In a case like yours
Some quiet country spot is a blessing. Well now, that's
My good news. – All the best!

MYRRHINE: And all the best to you!
    [*Exit* DAOS.]
PHILINNA: Why, what's the matter, child? Why do you
    walk about
    Wringing your hands like that?
MYRRHINE: How can I help it, though?
    I simply don't know what to do!
PHILINNA: Do about what?
MYRRHINE: About my daughter, Philinna. She's very near
    her time.

There are five other fragments from this play; four being parts of
speeches by Cleainetos, the farmer, to Gorgias, and one spoken by
Daos to the young man who doesn't want to marry his half-sister.
None of them gives any real clue as to what happened in the rest
of the play. The reader can therefore have the pleasure of working
out for himself the various possible lines of development which this
opening offers.

CLEAINETOS: I'm a rough countryman, I don't say other-
    wise.
    I don't know all the ins and outs of city ways.
    Still, I keep learning more and more as time goes on.

    This man, whoever he is, who has taken such unjust
    Advantage of your poverty, has in the same act
    Started a curse which may recoil on his own head.
    He may be well off; but his comfort's insecure;
    The stream of Fortune tends to change course overnight.

    A poor man, Gorgias, however sensibly
    He talks, always invites contempt; for people think
    His talk has one sole object: gain. The man who wears
    An old and shabby coat, even if he happens to be
    The injured party, is put down as a blackmailer.

Gorgias, the man of greatest strength is he who knows
How to endure the greatest wrongs with self-control.
This furious anger, this deep bitterness, betrays
At once to all the world mere pettiness of mind.

DAOS: Well, have you been struck by lightning? When
    you've managed to fall in love
With a free-born girl, you've not a word to say?
    Ridiculous!
You'll stand by and let them fix your wedding – with the
    wrong sweetheart?

THE SICYONIAN

CHARACTERS

The Speaker of the Prologue
CICHESIAS, an old Athenian
PHILUMENE, his daughter
STRATOPHANES, a young soldier
DROMON, a slave of Cichesias
THERON, Stratophanes' parasite
PYRRHIAS, Stratophanes' slave
MOSCHION, Stratophanes' brother
SMICRINES (?) and another man; an old man from Eleusis

★

Scene: Athens

This fragment is the most recently discovered. It is written on pieces of papyrus which were used as wrapping for an Egyptian mummy kept in a Paris museum, and the first transcript of it was published in 1964. Whereas other fragments of comparable length give us a whole scene or two or more, this manuscript gives us no whole scenes, but fairly long passages from several parts of the play. There are several passages where a part – the beginning or end – of each line is missing, but enough is left to convey the general sense; and here it has seemed worth while, for the sake of continuity, to write conjectural lines, which are indicated by square brackets.

Another difference between this and the other fragments is that here, in what the MS gives us, there is no sign of any moral issue such as forms the main theme of *The Arbitration*, *The Unkindest Cut*, and *The Samian Woman*; nor are there any passages of reflection on ethical or social topics such as form a large proportion of the smaller fragments found as quotations in other writers. In fact, three-quarters of what is left of *The Sicyonian* consists of narrative; part of it apparently from a Prologue, but most of it from a very long Messenger's Speech which is spoken to two characters about whom we know almost nothing. This speech, however, tells us something about Menander and his attitude to other dramatic writers; for it seems to be written as a sort of echo of the Messenger's Speech in Euripides' *Orestes*. There the Messenger recounts a meeting of the Argive Assembly to try Orestes and Electra for the murder of Clytemnestra; here the Messenger tells how an informally constituted assembly of Athenian citizens discuss who is to be legal guardian of an apparently orphan girl. Menander's narrative parallels that of Euripides in several features, notably in the opening passage, which was well known.

The central character of the play is Stratophanes, a young soldier who has just returned to Athens from military service in Asia Minor. He thinks he is a native of Sicyon, a town on the Corinthian Gulf, a little to the west of Corinth; but his supposed mother is a resident of Athens. On his arrival he sends his slave Pyrrhias ahead to break to her the news of his safe return; and Pyrrhias comes back saying that the 'mother' has died, and bringing with him her will, and a letter and a parcel that she left for Stratophanes. The letter tells him something about his parentage, and the parcel contains tokens to establish his identity. Stratophanes meets and falls in love with Philumene, who as an infant had been captured by pirates and sold in Asia Minor. Eventually both discover that they are of Athenian parentage, so that they can be legally married.

The first fragment is from the Prologue.

... I say that she was this man's daughter. When the
    pirates
Had all three in their power, they thought it not worth
    while
To carry off the old woman; but they took the child
And the slave to Mylasa, a Carian town, and offered them
For sale in the market. So this slave was sitting there
Holding his little mistress on one arm; when soon
A man called Hegemon, seeing they were for sale,
Came up and asked how much they were. He was told the
    price,
Agreed, and bought them. Another man, who was near
    this slave,
Brought there by the pirates to be sold at the same time,
Said, 'Cheer up, friend; this Sicyonian who has bought you
Is Hegemon, an excellent man, and very well off.'

The next passage begins with twenty-four lines each of which has
the first three, four, or five syllables missing; the complete lines start
at 'She didn't want you to live on ...'

THERON: Stay here; don't presume to ... There will be a
    time for that later on.
STRATOPHANES: By Zeus, you're quite right.
THERON: If you ... him he will fly into a rage; and then ...
STRATOPHANES: Let us agree on that. Now, by Zeus, I am
    resolved to stay here ...
THERON: I want no one else but you to have the benefit of
    what is yours ...
STRATOPHANES: Look, here he comes.
THERON: Who? ...
STRATOPHANES: Pyrrhias, whom I sent to my house to ...

and to say that we have arrived safely . . . I know [our return
will have been welcome] to my mother; then what can be the
reason that he is walking back slowly and looking downcast?
What news have you brought, Pyrrhias? Is my mother –?

PYRRHIAS: Your mother died last year.

STRATOPHANES: Died? Oh, Pyrrhias! I am sad to hear this.
She was very old.

PYRRHIAS: She, in fact, though, wasn't your mother; and
you're going to be involved,
Stratophanes, in tiresome business that you never reckoned
for.
You were not her son, apparently.

STRATOPHANES: Whose son am I then?

PYRRHIAS: Listen.
On her death-bed she wrote down the truth about your
birth. It's here.

[*He indicates a packet he is carrying.*]
People dying, they say, do all they can for those who go
on living.
She didn't want you to live on in ignorance of your family.
This was not the only thing, though. When your father
was alive
He lost a lawsuit – so it now appears – to some Boeotian.

STRATOPHANES: Yes, I heard.

PYRRHIAS: The sum involved was many talents, Stratophanes.

STRATOPHANES: News of all this reached me straight away
by letter, in Caria.
That same letter told me of my father's death.

PYRRHIAS: Your mother then
Learnt from legal experts that both you and all your
inheritance
Could be seized to pay this debt; so took this step to safeguard you,
And, since she was dying, restore you to your family, as
was right.

STRATOPHANES: Give me the letter.

PYRRHIAS: There. Look now, besides
the letter, I've brought these.
See, they're tokens; they'll identify you to your family;
So your mother used to say when she was alive – the people
who
Gave me these things said she did!

THERON: Divine Athene, make him yours!
So that he can have Philumene, and I can have Malthace!

STRATOPHANES: Come on, Theron!

THERON: You don't tell me –?

STRATOPHANES: This way; and stop talking, do!

THERON: Oh, all right, then; coming!

STRATOPHANES: Pyrrhias, you come too; and presently,
When I've told them, you'll produce the evidence, and
show it there
Large as life, for anybody who wants to see with his own
eyes.

Here the Scene ends. A performance 'Of the Chorus' follows; then
the next Scene begins. The speakers in this dialogue are not named;
I have called the first two A and B (A may possibly be named
Smicrines), and the third, the Old Man, since he is thus addressed
by B.

The first five lines of this Scene are complete; the next twenty-nine
are fragmentary; then seven or eight are missing; next, thirty-four
are fragmentary or missing; then come twenty-two complete lines;
and the rest of the scene is fragmentary.

A: You're just a fraud, a tiresome bagful of hot air,
If you think that a man who weeps and begs like that
Is telling the truth. Listen: behaviour of that kind
Is pretty well proof, these days, that the man's up to no
good.
You can't find out the truth that way. It's better to get
A few people to talk things over.

B: There you go –
  Rule by committee! You'd get away with robbery.

A: I swear my way's the better; and I'll stand by that.

B: Oh, you authoritarians! By Heracles,
  You drive me mad.

A: But why bellow abuse at me?

B: I hate you – yes, and your whole supercilious tribe!
  You're a public pest – as one day you'll admit.

A: Never!
  [I (suspect) you of stealing from the rich man his . . . and his
  equipment . . . Perhaps you don't actually carry the cash out
  of his house (but you abet) those who take it away . . .

B: Go to hell; you're full of hot air yourself.

A: If I had made you my fellow– . . .

    [An OLD MAN appears.]

B: Old man, stay here with us . . .

OLD MAN: Here I am. What is the subject of your loud
  dispute?

B: Wait to . . . a small . . .

A: We want to hear about . . .

OLD MAN: I happened to be (on my way) neither (from the
  country) nor, by Zeus, . . . (Someone), thinking he was doing
  me a favour, (told me there was a dispute going on; so, since
  I enjoy hearing about) other people's troubles – I'm a terrible
  man on a jury – . . . – and the backbone of the country they
  are, too.]
  Well, I had just come back from the city to meet the man
  From our village who'd got the job of sharing out
  A skinny half-sized bullock, and being told by those
  Who got the shares exactly what they thought of him –
  Well, I was one of them – I'm an Eleusinian,
  You see, from the deme of the Great Goddess. So I came,
  When I saw the crowd – 'Excuse me,' I said, and I got a
    place
  Right by the door. And there I saw this girl sitting;

And straight away, out of the people standing round
A sort of jury was constituted. [A man stood up
And said he was] legal guardian of the young girl.

Here seven or eight lines are missing, and three defective. Probably
the Old Man at this point tells of one or more others who took part
in the dispute about the girl; one must have been Dromon.

Well, that was what he did. And we all shouted out,
  'The girl's an Athenian citizen!' And even so
It was hard to quell the hubbub and make them quiet
  again.
When there was silence, we saw a young man – beardless,
  pale,
And smooth – go up to the slave and try to whisper to
  him.
We wouldn't let him. 'Speak up, louder!' There were
  shouts
Of 'What does he want?' 'Who is he?' 'What are you
  saying there?'
The youth replied, 'This slave knows well enough what
  I'm saying.'
Then a very manly-looking man . . . came forward . . . then
another man, and a third; and [when the first man] looked
closely [at the girl] he suddenly [poured forth] a stream [of
tears] and in a passion gripped [his hair] groaning. Those
who stood round were [astonished on seeing this].

When the MS resumes, the Old Man is telling what Stratophanes
(the 'manly-looking man') has said to the crowd.

'. . . [This man here, Dromon, was a slave] of the girl's
  father.
He's my slave now; therefore I give him back to her,
Renounce my claim to him, and want nothing in return.

Now let her find her father and her family;
I put no obstacle in her way.' 'Well said,' we cried.
'Now, gentlemen, hear my proposal. Since you yourselves
Are this girl's legal guardians – which she owes to me,
And now has nothing to fear – entrust her to the care
Of the priestess, and let *her* keep her on your behalf.'
These words won strong approval, as was fair. The crowd
All shouted, 'Quite right! Speak again!' So he went on,
'I used to think I too was a Sicyonian;
But now this man here, Pyrrhias, comes bringing me
My mother's will, and tokens establishing my birth.
And my belief is, if I can trust this document
And use it as proof, that I'm your fellow-citizen.
Don't rob me of this hope yet; but, if it is proved
That I too am a fellow-citizen of this girl
Whom I have brought back safe for her father, then let me
Ask him for her and marry her; and don't let any
Of my opponents get this girl into their power
Before her father appears.' 'Quite right!' 'Well said!'
    'Bravo!'
They shouted; 'Take her off to the priestess.' Suddenly
That pale-faced chap jumped up and said, 'Am I to believe
This man's got hold of a will from somewhere, just like
    that?
That he's your fellow-citizen? and that after this
Melodramatic abduction he'll just set her free?'
'Why don't you kill that smooth-face?' shouted everyone.
'It's you'll get killed, whoever you are,' the pale youth
    cries.
'You dangerous man,' says the soldier, 'crawl out of my
    reach.'
'All right, I'm going. Kindest regards to all!' – 'Come on,'
The soldier says to the girl, 'you can go.' The slave got up.
'She'll go, gentlemen,' says he, 'when *you* tell her to go.
So tell her.' – 'Very well; go!' Then she got up and went.

Well, that's as long as I stayed. What happened after that
I couldn't tell you; at that point I came away.

The next surviving passage gives only fragments of lines. From these
it is clear that it showed a recognition between a father, a mother,
and a son; and it seems likely that the son was Stratophanes. It
explains that his parents had sent him away in infancy to a foreign
woman. It seems too that the 'birth-tokens' which Pyrrhias brought
to Stratophanes figure in this scene; and just before the end of the
scene it transpires that Stratophanes is the brother of Moschion, the
beardless young man mentioned in the long narrative speech.

The final passage brings us nearly to the end of the play. The
opening situation here is puzzling; E. W. Handley convincingly
explains it by the suggestion that Theron has been trying to bribe
Cichesias to claim Philumene as his daughter, and so establish her as
an Athenian by birth; he refers to a clearly parallel situation in
Plautus' play *Poenulus*, which may well have owed some features
to Menander.

The name Scambonides means a member of the 'deme' of the
Scambonidae; this was one of the divisions of the Athenian citizen
body. The tradition said that Theseus had brought together the
various demes of Attica and united them in the single city of Athens.
The adjective *scambos* means 'bow-legged'; so Theron in adding the
description 'snub-nosed' is making what must have been a very
well-worn joke.

CICHESIAS: Go and hang yourself, you're a perfect pest!
    Get away from me!
  Do you imagine Cichesias would do such a thing?
  Or take money from anyone? What a monstrous trick!
  What, I? Cichesias? And a Scambonides?
THERON: That's just the point. So, take your pay – not now
    for what
  I said at first, but for this very thing.
CICHESIAS: What thing?
THERON: You are Cichesias.
CICHESIAS: Yes, and a Scambonides.

THERON: So much the better; you seem to have the hang of
the thing.

Be him! As it happens, you're snub-nosed, and short as
well,

As that slave said at the time.

CICHESIAS [*depressed*]:   I am the old man I am.

And add to that – at Halae I lost my little daughter

Of four years old; Dromon my slave too.

THERON: True enough,

You lost them.

CICHESIAS: Taken by pirates. You have reminded me

Of all that has gone wrong – all my sorrow and suffering.

THERON: Good! Now continue weeping for her – just like
that!

[*To Dromon*]: What a good-hearted man he is!

DROMON: Cichesias,

Your daughter, my young mistress, is in safe keeping . . .

[CICHESIAS: What do you say?

DROMON: I tell you again, your daughter's safe;

And I am Dromon your slave. I have looked after her

For all these years.

CICHESIAS: Can I believe you? Is this true?]

DROMON: She is alive, and she is here.

          [*Cichesias faints.*]

                              Cichesias!

Don't faint! Get up! – Theron, some water, water, quick!

THERON: By Zeus, I'll run in and get some. – Why, Stratophanes

Is indoors; I'll send him out to you.

DROMON: Don't bother now

About the water.

THERON: All the same I'll call him here.

DROMON: He's coming round. Hello, Cichesias!

CICHESIAS: What's all this?

Where am I? And what was it I heard someone say?

DROMON: You have your daughter, she's alive and safe.

CICHESIAS: Dromon,
Do you mean really safe, or just – alive?

DROMON: She's still
A virgin. No man has touched her.

CICHESIAS: Good.

DROMON: But you, master–
How are you?

CICHESIAS: I am alive, I can say that much, Dromon.
Beyond that – when you see an old, poor, lonely man,
Why, naturally, then everything must be all right.

[*Enter* STRATOPHANES *from the house; as he enters he
speaks to his mother who is indoors.*]

STRATOPHANES: I'll come back soon, mother, when I've
looked into this.

DROMON: Stratophanes, here's Philumene's father.

STRATOPHANES: Who is he?

DROMON: This man here.

STRATOPHANES: Greeting, father!

DROMON [*to Cichesias*]: This is the man who has saved
Your daughter.

CICHESIAS: May the gods make him a happy man!

STRATOPHANES: With your consent, father, I shall be happy
indeed
And richly blest.

[DROMON: Stratophanes, let's go at once
To the priestess and find Philumene.

STRATOPHANES: First I must go
Indoors and tell them . . .

DROMON: Come, Cichesias.

STRATOPHANES: Hey, Donax!
Donax, where are you? Go indoors and tell Malthace
To have my cases, bags and baskets – everything,
Brought to our neighbour's house. Tell Malthace herself
To go there, too; and bring the Carian slaves with you,

And Theron, and the donkeys. And I'll go myself
To see Philumene's father and arrange everything.
        [*They all move off. Enter* MOSCHION *alone.*]
MOSCHION: Moschion, as things are now, you'd better not
   so much
As glance at her. Just grin and bear it, Moschion.
What pure white skin she has! What lovely eyes! Ah, well!
My brother's a lucky bridegroom . . .
                        . . . And I shall be best man!

And may the noble, smiling maiden, Victory,
Bless all our ways, and stay our friend for evermore!]

SHORTER·FRAGMENTS

The fragments which follow are selected from the Loeb text edited by F. G. Allinson and are given the same numbering, which is taken from Kock's *Fragments of Attic Comedy-Writers*. The first thirty-three are from plays whose titles are known; the rest from unidentified plays.

From *The Robe-Bearer* or *The Flute-Girl*

65. If you've got sense, you won't give up your present life
    For matrimony. I'm married myself; and for that reason
    My advice to you is, Don't get married.

    Go on, then, marry; I wish you luck. You're setting sail
    On a real sea of trouble; not the Libyan Sea,
    Nor the Aegean, nor the Sicilian sandbanks, where
    Three ships perhaps in thirty may avoid shipwreck:
    In marriage no survivor has ever yet been known.

66. This Myrtile – you've only got to look at her,
    Or call out, 'Nurse!' – she'll rattle on and never stop.
    I tell you, it's easier to silence the bronze bell
    Of Dodona, which rings the whole day long, they say,
    If a passer-by just touches it, than to stop the tongue
    Of Myrtile; *she*'ll talk through the whole night as well.

From *The Superstitious Man*

109. A: Now send me a blessing, honoured gods! – Look: I
            was just
        Getting my shoes on, when my right-hand shoe-lace
        broke.

B: Of course it did, you nit-wit – it was rotten; and you
    Were too damned mean to buy yourself a decent pair.

Now, for example, take the Syrians.
Those people, every time they eat fish, by a kind
Of personal incontinence, begin to swell
In the feet and belly; then they dress themselves in
      sacking
And go and sit down in the road on a heap of dung,
And thus by extreme self-abasement they attempt
To propitiate the goddess.

From *The Bridesmaid*

114. Blessed is he that hath both money and common-sense;
     For such a man will use his money sensibly.

From *The Girl Twins*

118. He married off his daughter – he told me so himself –
     On thirty days' approval.

From *The Double Deceiver*

125. He whom the gods love dies young.

From *The Woman Set on Fire*

156. You think you're somebody, and you're proud of think-
     ing so.
     That's ruined a thousand others, and it'll ruin you.

From *The Promiser*

160. If you hold your own humble state in dignity,
　　　My friend, then others will respect it; but if you
　　　By holding it in contempt make it look humble, then
　　　In the world's eyes you'll be a self-made laughing-stock.

From *The Charioteer*

201. Look here: no god brings money and pours it in your
　　　　lap;
　　　But a god, if well-disposed, will find a way for you,
　　　Show you some opening that may lead to fortune.
　　　　Then,
　　　If you let that go, don't blame the god; it's time you
　　　　picked
　　　A quarrel with your yoke-mate – your own feebleness.

From *Thais*

217. This is the sort of girl I'd have you sing about,
　　　O Muse! – bold, ripe and lovely, hard to contradict;
　　　Who'll jilt you, lock you out, never stop wheedling
　　　　you,
　　　Never love anyone, never stop pretending to.

218. The thing that spoils good character is bad company.

From *The Possessed Woman*

223. If some god were to come to me and say, 'Craton,
　　　After your death you shall have your life over again;

You shall be whatever you choose – dog, sheep, goat,
   man, or horse;
You're to have a second life; that is decreed by
   Fate,
So make your choice – ' I think I'd answer straight
   away,
'Anything but a man. Man's the sole living creature
Whose good fortune and bad are allotted him unfairly.
A first-rate horse, for example, 's much more carefully
Looked after than another; if you're a good dog
You're valued much more than a bad one. A thorough-
   bred cock
Lives on a special diet; an inferior one
Is even afraid of a better cock. But a good man,
A man of birth and breeding – in this age of ours
Gets no advantage whatsoever. Bum-suckers –
They come off best of any; blackmailers come next;
Slanderers a good third. Better be born a donkey
Than see your inferiors living in better style than you.'

From *The Treasure*

235. Then is not Eros the most mighty of all gods,
   And the most honoured? Why, there's not a living
   man
   So sunk in meanness, so cut-and-dried in all his ways,
   As not to give up some share of his livelihood
   To Eros. Now, if Eros treats you kindly, then
   He makes you act like this while you're still young; but
   if
   You're one of those who put it off till they've grown
   old,
   You'll pay your dues with interest for the time you've
   lost.

From *Thrasyleon*

240. This 'Know Yourself' is a silly proverb in some ways;
 To know the man next door's a much more useful rule.

From *The Doorkeeper*

923. It's no joke, to plunge into a family dinner-party, where
 First papa leads off the speeches, cup in hand, and gives
  them all
 Pointed good advice; mama comes second; then a
  grandmother
 Rambles on a little; then great-uncle, in a growling
  bass;
 Then comes some old lady who alludes to you as 'dear-
  est boy'.
 All the time you nod your head and beam at them . . .

From *The Priestess*

245. Madam, no god helps one man at another's prayer.
 If man, by clashing cymbals, can deflect a god
 To his own will, this makes him greater than the god.
 Such theories are invented by unscrupulous men
 To brazen out a living; fabrications which
 Make human life a mockery.

From *The Carthaginian*

261. No man knows who his own father is; but all of us
 Make some assumption about it, or hold some belief.

It is no easy matter in a single day
To change a habit of folly deep ingrained by time.

From *The Guitar-Player*

A father speaks:
And now what can this mean? It's not at all like *him*!
Moschion sends and asks me to come up to town.
In the past, if ever I happened to be in town
He'd shoot off to the country; and if I went there
He'd come back here again – and drink. Well, fair
   enough;
No father here to tell him how to behave. Mind you,
I never get angry with him; I myself was one
Of those who have a gift for running short of
   money.
That's one thing I can't blame my wife for; it's a gift
He got from me. Anyway, the boy's doing no good.
Better go in and see if he's here; and if he's not
I'll go straight to the market-place. I'll find him there,
I know, somewhere in Hermes Street.

I used to think once, Phanias, that wealthy men,
Having no need to borrow money, never lie
Awake at night, groaning and tossing up and down,
Saying, What shall I do? but fall into a sweet
And gentle sleep, leaving such tortures to the poor.
But now I see that you who are called the lucky ones
Have troubles just like ours. In fact, trouble itself
Is twin brother to life. When life holds luxury,
Trouble's there too; when life brings fame, there's still
   trouble;
And if you're poor, trouble grows old along with
   you.

From *The Pilots*

301. Take money, now: do you, young man, regard it as
     Useful for buying just the daily necessities –
     Bread, flour, vinegar, oil – or more important things?
     Money can't buy you immortality, not if
     You gathered in one heap all the gold of Tantalus.
     You'll die and leave all that to others. See what I mean?
     However rich you are, don't pin your faith to wealth;
     And what's more, don't look down on us because we're
       poor.
     Prove to the world, each day, that you deserve your
       luck.

302. A bachelor speaks:
     What chatterers we are, we wretched suffering men,
     All of us so blown up about ourselves! Why, men
     Don't know the nature of their own kind. Now, there's
       a man –
     You look at him in the street, and call him fortunate;
     But once he opens his front door – poor wretch! His
       wife
     Rules the whole roost, gives orders, quarrels day and
       night.
     He suffers a thousand agonies; I suffer none!

From *Drunkenness*

319. Like offering, like fortune, that's the truth of it.
     Suppose I bring to the gods a wretched sheep that cost
     A bare ten drachmas, and then spend nearly a talent on
     Flute-girls, guitar-girls, scented oil, expensive wine
     From Mende or Thasos, eels, and honey, and cheese;
       so that

I can claim in honesty to receive ten drachmas'
    worth
Of blessing, if the sacrifice proves acceptable,
And if it doesn't, on top of all there's a fine to pay—
Doesn't sacrificing let me in for a double loss?
If I were a god I'd forbid them ever to lay the rump
On the altar unless they dedicated the eel as well –
As a fee for the death of their rich uncle Callimedon.

From *The Necklace*

402. From today on my heiress-wife will sleep at ease,
    Whichever side she lies on. A great deed's been done,
    A notable deed. She's bundled out of the house – the
      way
    She wanted to – that woman who got under her skin,
    So that everyone may gaze on the face of Crobyle,
    And she be known as my wife, mistress of the house.
    As for that face which she's the proud possessor of –
    You know the saying about 'a donkey among apes'? –
    Well, there you are. What I could say about that night
    When this disaster started! – but I won't. Oh, gods!
    To think I married Crobyle – ten thousand pounds
    For dowry, and a nose just eighteen inches long.
    Am I to let her snort me off like that? By Zeus,
    Lord of Olympus, and by Athene, I will not.
    A nice, obedient little girl – and Crobyle
    Must whip her off like that before you could say knife!

From *The Soldiers*

447.   When you're in any difficulty,
    Go off alone and think about it. Good ideas

Don't come with shouting; but they show up clear
  enough
When a man sits down and reasons things out by himself.

From *Trophonius*

462. This dinner is for entertaining a visitor.
  What visitor? Where's he from? That makes a difference
  To a Cook, you know. Now, take these fancy visitors
  From the islands, reared on fresh-caught fish from far
    and near –
  They don't find sea-food all that wonderful; to them
  It's just a side-dish. Seasoned stuffing, savoury sauce –
  That's what those gentry go for. Now, an Arcadian –
  He's different; doesn't live by the sea; what fetches
    him
  Is limpets. Then there's your Ionian: rich and coarse.
  Thick soup I give him; Lydian hot-pot; tasty stews
  Flavoured with Aphrodisiac herbs.

From *The Changeling*, or *The Rustic*

481.   I'll tell you, Parmenon,
  Who seems to me to have the happiest life: the man
  Who takes a steady look at the majestic sights
  Our world offers – the common sun, stars, water, clouds,
  Fire; and having seen them, and lived free from pain, at
    once
  Goes back to where he came from. These same sights
    will be, .
  If you live to a hundred, always there, always the same;
  And equally if you die young; but you will never

See more majestic sights than these. Think of this time
I speak of, as a people's festival, or as
A visit to some city, where you stand and watch
The crowds, the streets, the thieves, the gamblers, and
　the way
People amuse themselves. If you go back early
To your lodging, you'll have money in your pocket, and
No enemies. The man who stays too long grows tired,
Loses what he once had, gets old, wretched, and poor,
Wanders about, makes enemies, or falls a prey
To plotters; till at last an ignominious death
Sends him off home.

482. Stop talking about 'mind'; the mind of man can do
　　　Nothing. It is Chance (has Chance a 'mind' or a 'holy
　　　　spirit'?)
　　　– Whatever you call it, Chance steers, governs, and
　　　　preserves
　　　Everything. Human forethought is all smoke, all bilge.
　　　It's true – you take my word; you'll never say I'm
　　　　wrong.
　　　Each single thought, each word, each act of ours is just
　　　Chance. All you and I can do is sign on the dotted line.

483. Chance steers the world. You talk of 'brains', 'wisdom':
　　　you're wrong.
　　　'Chance', you should say – unless you love meaningless
　　　　words.

From *The Ghost*

A summary[1] of the plot of this play has survived, and the substance
of it is as follows:

　1. This summary is quoted from F. C. Allinson's edition of Menander in
the Loeb Library, page 448.

A young man has a stepmother who, before she married his father, has had by a neighbour a daughter. The maiden, whom she wishes to have continually with her, is brought up secretly in the adjoining house, and the party wall between the neighbour's and her husband's house is pierced by a passage with its entrance made to resemble a shrine which she covers with garlands and boughs. Under the pretext of ritual performances she is able to enjoy regular visits from her daughter. The young woman, however, is seen by the stepson, who at first is terrified, as he takes the maiden for a ghost. Further encounters change terror into love, and a happy marriage is arranged with the consent of all parties concerned.

In the first of these fragments a 'household divinity', probably the god worshipped at the make-believe shrine, is explaining the situation to the audience.

Now, she is no ghost, but a real girl of flesh and blood,
And daughter to this married woman, who long ago
Had this child by a neighbour, and disposed of her,
Before she came here, to a nurse to keep and rear.
The girl now lives with this nurse in the house next door.
Whenever the husband is at home, the girl is kept
Indoors and closely guarded; but at other times,
When he's away at sea and there's less need for care,
She leaves the house she lives in usually, and appears
Here. Now I'm sure you all want to know exactly how
This apparition comes. Her mother has made a hole
Right through the wall, so both of them can keep an eye
On everything; this doorway is completely hidden
With wreaths and branches, so that no one coming in
Would see it; there's an altar to the goddess too.

The young man in the story, the stepson Pheidias, has to be told a few home-truths by a family slave before he can qualify to win the girl.

SLAVE: What price does wheat fetch in the market nowadays?

PHEIDIAS: Why, what's that got to do with you?

SLAVE: Nothing. I just
   Wanted to use the subject to point out a truth.
   If wheat is dear, just worry a bit on *my* account –
   I'm poor. Remember, Pheidias, not only you
   Are human, but an unhappy man is human too.
   Don't crave for things beyond your reach. You say you
      have
   Insomnia. Why? Examine the sort of man you are,
   And you'll learn why. You take a stroll to the market-
      place;
   Soon you come back; and if your legs are tired you take
   A comfortable bath; after your bath you bolt a meal
   Ad lib. Your whole life's one long doze. To sum it up:
   There's nothing wrong with you; your only illness is
   The luxurious way you've spent your life. – A coarse
      expression,
   Master, occurs to me – forgive me – as they say,
   You're so packed round with blessings, you don't know
      where to shit;
   And that's the truth.

PHEIDIAS: I hope you die before next year!

SLAVE: I swear it's the plain truth I've told you. Your
      disease
   Is this and nothing else.

PHEIDIAS: But, damn it all, I'm ill!
   I'm really ill!

SLAVE: Your folly is just feebleness
   And self-indulgence.

PHEIDIAS: Say it is, then: what do you think
   I ought to do? You seem to have this all worked out.

SLAVE: You want my advice? Then you shall have it,
      Pheidias.
   If you had any real complaint you'd have to find
   A real cure for it; but you haven't – it's a sham.

Well, then, find a sham remedy for it. Just pretend
That something's doing you good. Get all the women
   slaves
Round in a ring, and let them massage you all over
And fumigate you. Get some water from three springs,
Put in some salt and peas, and sprinkle it over you . . .

FRAGMENTS FROM UNIDENTIFIED
PLAYS

531. Young master, if when your mother brought you into
    the world
    You were born the only one on earth to do as you liked
    All through your life, and still be always fortunate –
    If some god made an arrangement with you on these
    terms,
    You're rightly indignant; he's deceived you; it's
    outrageous.
    But if you breathe this common air of heaven – to use
    A phrase that smacks of Tragedy – on the self-same
    terms
    As all of us, then you must bear this trouble with
    A better courage. Reason with yourself. The long
    And short of the whole matter is, you are a man;
    And there's no creature living that can suffer change –
    Up to the top or down to the depth – more rapidly
    Than a man. And very rightly; man himself is weak,
    But handles mighty matters; when he falls, he brings
    Much that is excellent down with him to the dust.
    Now you, young master – what were those good things
    you've lost?
    Nothing extraordinary; and the troubles you have now
    Are merely average; bear them, then, and keep your
    balance.

532. The right way to go marrying, by Saviour Zeus,
    Is the same way you go shopping. You shouldn't
    haggle over
    Irrelevant details – who was the girl's grandfather,
    Or grandmother – while giving never a thought or look

To the character of the bride herself, the woman you
    mean
To live with; and what's the use of hurrying off to the
    Bank
With her dowry-money, to get the Banker to test the
    coin –
Which won't stay in the house five months – if you
    don't apply
A single test to the woman who's going to settle down
In your house for the rest of your life, but take
    haphazard
An inconsiderate, quarrelsome, difficult wife, who even
May be a talker.
              I shall take my own daughter round
The whole city: 'You who want to marry this girl,' I'll
    say,
'Just chat with her; find out beforehand the true
    measure
Of the pest that you're acquiring. A woman *is* a pest –
That can't be helped; the luckiest man's the one who
    gets
The least unbearable pest.'

533. A daughter speaks:
Family? I'm fed up with this talk of 'family'.
Mother, don't – if you love me – every time I mention
A man, start talking about his family. People who
Haven't a single good quality to call their own –
They are the ones who talk like that of family,
Or titles, or decorations; reel off grandfathers
One after the other, and that's all they've got. Can you
Tell me of a man who hasn't got grandfathers? or how
A man could be born without them? People who, for
    one
Reason or another – living abroad, or losing friends –

241

Can't name their grandfathers – are they any worse born
   than those
Who can? Mother, if a man has a noble character
Which prompts him to a good life, then he's of noble
   birth,
Even if he's a black African. And you 'don't like
Scythians'? To hell! Wasn't Anacharsis[1] a Scythian?

534. Animals enjoy a life that's full of blessings – and
   They've much more sense than men have. Take this
     donkey here:
A donkey's an unfortunate beast, we all agree;
None of his troubles come to him by his own fault,
He has them all by Nature's gift. But we, apart
From troubles which are inevitable, must needs
   invent
Others ourselves. Schemes, reputations, rivalries,
Laws – all these curses men have added to Nature's ills.

535. So, now you see how just it is that pictures show
   Prometheus always nailed up on a rock; and he has
A torch-race – that's his only honour; nothing else.
Why? He created, what all gods must surely loathe:
Women. You honoured gods, what a hateful race they
   are!
Is there any man here who's going to marry? I said
   'marry'.
From then on, evil concupiscence will be his life's
Secret story: an adulterer wallowing in his bed;
The poison-trade; and that worst of all sicknesses,
Which a woman lives with all her life long – jealousy.

  1. A Scythian of royal rank, who early in the sixth century B.C. visited
Athens and became a friend of Solon the Athenian law-giver, and was widely
admired for his wisdom.

536. A young man addresses the audience:
By Athene, gentlemen, I can't find a metaphor
To illustrate what has happened – what's demolishing me
All in a moment. I turn things over in my mind.
A tornado, now: the time it takes to wind itself up,
Get nearer, hit you, then tear off – why, it takes an age.
Or a gale at sea; but there, you've breathing-space to
shout
'Zeus save us!' or 'Hang on to those ropes!' or to wait
For the second monster wave, and then the third, or try
To get hold of a bit of wreckage. But with me – oh, no!
One touch, one single kiss – I'd had it, I was sunk.

537. Epicharmus[1] tells us that the gods are: water, wind,
Earth, fire, the sun, the stars. But I've got an idea
The useful gods for you and me are silver and gold.
Put up a shrine at home for those two; pray to them.
What do you long for? You shall have it all: estates,
Houses and servants; silverware; friends; jurymen;
Witnesses. Pay – that's all: you'll have the gods them-
selves
Your obedient servants.

540. Perhaps, young man, it's never struck you that every-
thing
Goes rotten by a corruption that's peculiar to it;
Each thing's corruption originates within itself.
For instance, look at rust – the way it eats up iron;
Or moths eat woollen cloaks, or woodworms devour
wood.
Just so, the most evil of all evil things, envy,
Causes consumption of the soul; it always has,
And always will; envy, the impious tendency
Of a wicked heart.

1. A Pythagorean philosopher, and writer of comedies, 540–450 B.C.

541. This passion of love – have you ever wondered where it
finds
Its origin? What actual thing enslaves a man?
A face? Nonsense, if that were so, all men would fall
For the same girl. If merely looking makes the choice,
All men have equal eyes. Or, is what draws men on
As lovers, the pleasure a woman gives in intercourse?
If so, then why does one man leave her bed heart-whole
And go off laughing at her, while another's caught for
life?
This sickness of man's heart lies in the crux of time;
And when you're wounded, the blow's dealt inside
yourself.

542. If each of us would willingly take our part, and join
In stout resistance, call each unjust act a blow
Aimed at ourselves no less than at our neighbour, if
We worked and fought in common, we wouldn't every
time
See crime succeed; we'd keep a watch on wicked men,
Get them their just deserts; and soon they'd be reduced
To a mere handful, easily kept under control.

545. 'Demonstration'[1] is my name; Truth and Outspoken-
ness
Are friends of mine, and Freedom is my first cousin.
The only mortals I'm an enemy to are those
Who fear my tongue. I know everything; and what I
know
About your secrets, I unfold in clear detail.
To me, a fig's a fig; I call a spade a spade.

1. The Greek word translated 'demonstration' is one used in English as a
term in Logic – 'elenchus'. It means 'proof' provided by the demonstration
or uncovering of facts which constitute evidence.

549. Being mortal, never pray for an untroubled life;
But ask the gods to give you an enduring heart.
For if you want to live your whole life free from pain
You must become either a god or else a corpse.
Consider other men's troubles; that will comfort yours.

551. A man whose heart is sound finds Fortune his ally.
Every man is attended from the hour of birth
By a spirit to guide him through the mysteries of life –
A good spirit. We should not believe that there exists
Any evil spirit inflicting harm on human lives
Or evil in its own nature; but that every god
Is himself good. People of evil character
Who have made a tangle of their own lives, or ruined
  those
Of others by their folly – these are the people who
Say it's God's doing, and blame God for their own
  fault.

552. Old age, our human body's enemy, you thief
Of beauty's moulded treasures, who re-draw the clean
Contour of manly limbs to make it ugliness,
And change swiftness of foot to endless faltering!

554. We all from time to time – isn't this true, father? –
Turn from our drinking, from our pleasures of every
  day,
And seek someone to share the heart's core of our life.
And every man is sure he has found a marvellous
Treasure, if he gains even the semblance of a friend.

560. At family prayers there's always one thing I leave out:
I never pray for harmony in domestic life.
There are times in every household when a spontaneous
Feud between servants can be a most useful thing.

572. When you engage in an honest undertaking, hold
    Good hope as a shield before you, and be sure that God
    Himself lends strength to boldness in a righteous cause.

594. It's clear Fortune can have no bodily existence; but
    Those who can't bear the natural course of life's events
    Call by the name of Fortune their own character.

595. It's always so: your saved man is a thankless thing.
    Offer help – and that moment all the gratitude
    Which he, when helpless, swore he'd feel for ever, dies.

620. It seems to me sheer folly, my Philumene,
    To have all the perception that one ought to have
    And then not guard against what one ought to guard
      against.

627. If you observe, it's not the number of cups that makes
    A man drunk, but the character of the man who drinks.

632. When a man bears a secret guilt, however bold
    He may be, conscience makes him very cowardly.

638. I'm rather young; but when I speak, don't think of
      that;
    Just notice if I'm speaking like a man of sense.

639. It's not white hair that makes a man intelligent;
    Some people have a mind that's naturally mature.

659. Don't cause your father any distress; the man who loves
    You most is angered too by the most trivial things.

690. I hate the poor man who brings presents to the rich.
    It just makes clear to everyone how starved he is.

698. Slave, if you're slave to one who was born a slave, look
     out:
     The freed ox never remembers what the yoke was like.

702. To teach a woman to write is not a good idea;
     You might as well feed poison to a deadly snake.

704. Don't offer your wife even the very best advice.
     She'll take her own, and for her pleasure do her worst.

745.   ... But a woman who pays you compliments
     Is really something to be afraid of.

760. There's one slave of the whole household, and that's the
     master of it.

767. I hate a bad man when he speaks what's honourable.

*Some other Penguin Classics
are described on the
following pages*

HOMER

THE ILIAD

Translated by E. V. Rieu

The Greeks considered the *Iliad* their greatest literary achievement, and no epic poem in any language has ever rivalled it. Out of a single episode in the Tale of Troy, Achilles' withdrawal from the fighting and his return to kill the Trojan hero Hector, Homer created a timeless dramatic tragedy. His characters are heroic but their passions and problems are human and universal, and he presents them with compassion, understanding, and humour against the harsh background of war.

E. V. Rieu's prose translation has the same direct simplicity and subtle elegance which distinguishes his *Odyssey*; it moves swiftly and confidently through the greater complexity of the *Iliad* and never falls short of the nobility of Homer's theme.

EURIPIDES

MEDEA AND OTHER PLAYS

Translated by Philip Vellacott

Four more plays by Euripides (484–407 B.C.) are
presented in this volume in modern English by
Philip Vellacott, who has already translated many of
the great Greek dramas for the Penguin Classics.

  Medea, the story of that princess's horrible revenge
for the infidelity of Jason, the hero of the Argonauts,
is Euripides' earliest surviving tragedy, whilst
Heracles is among his latest plays. In *Hecabe* and
Electra he again underlines the wickedness of revenge.
An outspoken critic of society and the gods, Euripides
was at his most eloquent on the theme of human suffering, and among the most lyrical of all poets.

XENOPHON
A HISTORY OF MY TIMES

Translated by Rex Warner

A History of My Times which opens with the final defeat of Athens at the hands of Lysander takes up the story of the Peloponnesian War at the point at which Thucydides broke off. Xenophon, an exile, was neither such a perfect historian nor such a stalwart Athenian as Thucydides, and his strangely sentimental and uncritical regard for Sparta seemed to blind him to the subsequent recovery made by Athens. Nevertheless his simple soldierly record of the Spartan and Theban hegemonies, culminating in the indecisive battle of Mantinea (362 B.C.), does underline the profound effects of the tragic Peloponnesian War.

SOPHOCLES

ELECTRA AND OTHER PLAYS

Translated by E. F. Watling

This volume contains four plays by Sophocles
(496–406 B.C.) who was the first to give to ancient
Greek drama a structure recognizably related to its
modern descendant. In *Electra* he objectively presents
part of the Oresteian legend, while *Woman of
Trachis* is remarkable for the human verisimilitude
imparted to a near-repulsive piece of mythology.
Philoctetes portrays the struggles of right against
might, and *Ajax* takes for its theme that of the great
man fallen. E. F. Watling also translated Sophocles'
The Theban Plays for the Penguin Classics.

AESCHYLUS

THE ORESTEIAN TRILOGY

Translated by Philip Vellacott

What is justice? How is it related to vengeance? Can justice be reconciled with the demands of religion, the violence of human feeling, the forces of Fate?

These questions, which puzzled thoughtful Athenians in the decades after the battle of Marathon, provided the theme for the *Agamemnon*, *The Choephori*, and *The Eumenides* those grim tragedies that make up the Oresteian Trilogy. In these plays Aeschylus (525–456 B.C.) takes as his subject the bloody character of murder and revenge within the royal family of Argos – a chain finally broken only by the intervention of the goddess Athene. Philip Vellacott's verse translation makes available to the modern reader a milestone in the history of drama.